D1798637

WORLD WAR II
Dispatches to Akron

AN AIRMAN'S LETTERS HOME

CHRISTOPHER M. LAHURD

Based on war letters written by Daniel E. LaHurd

THE
History
PRESS

Published by The History Press
Charleston, SC
www.historypress.net

Copyright © 2009 by Christopher M. LaHurd
The History Press edition 2017
All rights reserved
Originally published as *A Story of One: Walking the Path of a World War II Airman*
by Merriam Press in 2009.

ISBN 9781540214065

Library of Congress Control Number: 2016953506

Notice: The information in this book is true and complete to the best of our knowledge. It is offered without guarantee on the part of the author or The History Press. The author and The History Press disclaim all liability in connection with the use of this book.

All rights reserved. No part of this book may be reproduced or transmitted in any form whatsoever without prior written permission from the publisher except in the case of brief quotations embodied in critical articles and reviews.

CONTENTS

Acknowledgements 7
Foreword, by Stanton Michael Rickey,
    Lieutenant Colonel, USAF (Retired) 9
Introduction 11

1. Memmingen Raid 15
2. Bouncing Betty 28
3. Airborne 44
4. Square One 56
5. Eye on Norden 67
6. Flying Bookkeepers 83
7. Roses and Rivets 94
8. Groom Deploys 101
9. Over the Deep Blue Pond 113
10. Last Repose 133
11. Nazi Interview 138
12. The Dash 148
13. *Stalag Luft I* 154
14. Lost Boys 161
15. Monotony 168
16. Lucky 184
17. Bombardier's Promise 192
18. Victory Garden 195
19. One Life 197

Writer's Note 201
Bibliography 203
About the Author 207

Dedicated to my grandfather
Daniel Elias LaHurd

ACKNOWLEDGEMENTS

Thanks to my grandmother Madeline LaHurd; this heroine's hardships and tireless efforts between 1939 and 1945 were fascinating and admirable. To Stanton "Mike" Rickey, Fred Hicks and the entire 483rd Bombardment Association for welcoming me with open arms. These brave men shaped our country into a stronger and richer nation. They are true heroes, and their stories will never be forgotten by me. To Patti Russo, for an excellent editing job; her thoughtful input and keen eye were extraordinary. To Ryan LaHurd and Jeff LaHurd for their opinions, suggestions and criticisms; I am extremely grateful for their help. To my parents, Denny and Karen; sister, Megan; and wife, Courtney, for their unremitting support; each one of them provided me with the boost that I needed to complete this book. To all of the LaHurds, for the tidbits of information that I learned from them in brief conversation; their stories helped me to congeal an accurate and hopefully interesting story.

FOREWORD

This narrative about Daniel LaHurd's personal experiences during World War II is unique in that it recounts a story of one individual. This riveting memoir offers much insight into the extensive training process that transforms a raw recruit into a highly professional member of a wartime bomber aircrew. We learn of his feelings about the conflict and the interruption of peacetime family life that so many soldiers endured.

In one sense, LaHurd's story is everyman's in microcosm yet also unique in chronicling those experiences shared by so many others who fought the good fight and carried the war deep into the heartland of Nazi Germany. The Strategic Air War Campaign brought devastation to the enemy industrial and infrastructure complex and played a leading role in achieving America's ultimate victory.

Can you imagine what it was like in World War II when the sky on a given day was filled with five hundred or even as many as one thousand B-17s and B-24s heading toward enemy targets? Add to that accompanying P-51, P-47 and P-38 fighter escorts, and you can envision an air armada on a massive scale such as the world has never seen, before or since.

The air war in Europe was a killing field. *Luftwaffe* fighter planes and enemy antiaircraft flak gunners exacted a heavy toll in defense of their homeland. The U.S. Army Air Forces in Europe lost a total of seven thousand heavy bombers destroyed in combat and nearly four thousand fighter planes. Over 200,000 American airmen flew in combat with the Eighth and Fifteenth Air Forces in Europe. The fatality rate among bomber aircrews exceeded that of the ground forces in Europe. The odds of successfully completing a tour of duty were estimated at one in three. The U.S. Air Force had more killed and wounded than the U.S. Marine Corps suffered in all the amphibious landings in the Pacific combined. Among these bomber crews, some 30,000 American airmen were killed in action, 14,000 wounded and 33,000 more were captured after parachuting from stricken aircraft or crash landing in enemy territory. They spent the rest of the war as POWs in Nazi prison camps.

Christopher LaHurd provides a detailed description of the path that most POWs took after capture. From all over Europe, they were initially sent to a central intelligence center at Dulag Luft near Frankfurt to endure solitary confinement and interrogation. Subsequently, they were transferred to a permanent stalag. The author gives a superb description of prison camp life. We learn of the camaraderie among men coping with bleak prospects yet determined to survive under arduous circumstances and their elation when liberated at war's end. Homecoming and resumption of peacetime activities were all the more rewarding as a result of their sharpened appreciation gained from the hardship and sacrifices they endured.

—Stanton Michael Rickey, Lieutenant Colonel, USAF (Retired)
B-17 Pilot, 817th Squadron, 483rd Bombardment Group,
also shot down at Memmingen, Germany, on July 18, 1944

INTRODUCTION

The death of one man is a tragedy. The death of millions is a statistic.
—*Joseph Stalin*

All too often we think of wars on a massive scale: tons of explosives, thousands of men, billions of dollars and death tolls in the thousands, hundreds of thousands or millions. While watching the news, reading the paper or listening to the radio, how many of us really think about the individual combatant behind the headline? What if you were fond of, or familiar with, just one soldier? What if you knew the story of that soldier's life? Would you have a different perspective on that war? Would a soldier's death still be a statistic, or would it be something more?

The Second World War began with a treaty gone wrong and a German blitzkrieg. After six years, the war concluded with atomic blasts over two Japanese cities. The greatest war known to mankind left a mosaic of cultural, political and militaristic changes after its conclusion in 1945. Ramifications of this war still linger today, from the transformation of international borders to the creation of the atomic age, the development of new jurisprudences and the implementation of NATO and the United Nations.

It is estimated that fifty-seven million human lives were lost during the war.* When using such large numbers, the scope becomes unfathomable; the ability to grasp that death toll becomes even more difficult. If one knew

---

* Estimates for the Second World War's total death toll range from forty million to seventy million people.

the individual story of every combatant and civilian who experienced World War II, fifty-seven million would be a terribly sad yet heroic statistic.

The individual soldier should never be forgotten in the sterile numbers attempting to measure a world war, for they were the catalyst of the outcome. Moreover, one would realize the courage, honor and strength of these soldiers, their families and all other civilians caught in the middle. My pursuit is to tell the story of one American airman and his daily activities during the war, with the hope that this information can be extrapolated, helping the reader grasp the sacrifices made by millions of people during the years 1939–45.

A twenty-three-three-year-old American boy stood in line to sign his name at the local recruiting station for the United States Army Air Force in February 1942.* Only two months previously, Japanese naval and air forces had attacked Pearl Harbor. Although the attack had occurred thousands of miles away, the boy from Akron, Ohio, felt directly affected. Saddened and enraged, he determined he would soon be an airman who would avenge the deaths of the Americans killed on December 7.

Although Daniel Elias LaHurd was not named in the history books like Dwight Eisenhower, George Patton, Douglas MacArthur, Omar Bradley and George Marshall, his service was just as vital. All Americans—farmer, factory worker, engineer and housewife—played a critical role in the United States' victory in World War II. Daniel LaHurd's was in the air above enemy territory. As totalitarian governments led by fascist dictators fueled the war in Europe and the Pacific, he scribbled his signature on the bottom line of recruitment papers. His new life was about to begin.

A few weeks after my grandfather Daniel Elias LaHurd passed away in the early fall of 2005, a large cardboard box was delivered to my house. The return address read Sarasota, Florida, the city my grandfather resided in after living in the Akron, Ohio area for nearly forty years after the war. I carefully cut the tape that was holding the top flaps of the box and tried to guess what was inside. A dark walnut chest sat amid crumpled-up newspaper. When I opened the chest and saw the creased picture of my grandfather in his military uniform resting atop a stack of aged and yellowed letters, I knew instantly what they were. My eyes filled with tears.

---

* On June 20, 1941, the United States Army Air Corps (USAAC) became the United States Army Air Force (USAAF).

My grandfather had become my best friend, hero and confidant during the twenty-three years that I was able to spend with him. During those years, I had asked my grandfather many questions about his military days and had received only very brief answers followed by a quick change of subject. Most of my questions were answered with a "yes" or "no" or "it was no big deal" or "just doing my duty," or he would say, with tears in his eyes, "those were good men, good soldiers." I knew very little about this hidden part of my grandfather's life. I wanted to know more, but he would never give me more. Fearful of bringing back nightmares or grief, I never pried and never pushed. But now, the walnut box sitting in front of me possessed his life from 1942 to 1945—a part of his life that I thought had died with him.

As I was reading and organizing these letters, I found myself catapulted back to the 1940s. The language and firsthand accounts acted as a time machine. The small facts sometimes were the most interesting; for example, the language used during this time, the activities of interest, the day-to-day wants and needs of a GI, the costs of living and the emotions of being away from home for years. I began to imagine myself in the same position and became gripped with suspense as I read each new letter, even though I knew how the story turned out. I realized that these letters and this story must be shared with others.

That was the start of *World War II Dispatches to Akron*. This book is based on my grandfather's letters, the actual letters of an American World War II bombardier. Nearly every day was accounted for or written about for three years as Daniel attempted to inform his parents, sister, brothers and, later, his wife about his new life and increasing responsibilities. Every day was a new adventure to the airman.

This book is not intended to lionize a man whom I consider a hero, my grandfather, but to re-create a straightforward story of a young cadet set on adventure who grew into a mature lieutenant and thoughtful man. I hope that this very personal, singular story will in some way make real the stories of all other soldiers who fought or are fighting in wars past and present.[*]

---

[*] All letters within this book are transcribed as written and unedited.

Chapter 1

MEMMINGEN RAID

July 18, 1944

Hitler may have built a fortress around Europe,
but he forgot to put a roof on it.
—*President Franklin Roosevelt*

On the early morning of July 18, 1944, the air was damp and a cool breeze twisted through the hills and fields of Memmingen, Germany, sixty-four miles west of Munich, in the southwestern part of the country. Spread across the foothills of the Alps, the region was made up of small forests and stretches of farmland that had been tended for centuries by villagers who lived in remote cottages and isolated small towns.

As the sun gradually rose over the horizon, splashing the land with the first rays of light, the large, looming site of a German military air base rose out of the disappearing darkness, looking out of place in the bucolic expanse of greenery surrounding it. As the sun grew over the hills, winged silhouettes were cast across tarmacs. Nazi aerodrome and military installations sprawled over the landscape: fighter planes, bombers, hangars, warehouses, barracks and repair sheds showed Germany's efforts to maintain a forceful flying power.

A short distance away from the tarmacs, inside a reinforced concrete barracks, a blond-haired, blue-eyed *unteroffizier** of the German *Luftwaffe* was awakened at dawn. The exterior walls of his barracks were stained with

---

* *Unteroffizier* is a rank comparable to a United States staff sergeant.

black soot from continuous Allied bombing missions attempting to destroy the installation. The rising light revealed shadowed craters throughout the walls of the different buildings. Accelerated debris blown in all directions from exploding bombs and .50-caliber bullets had chipped away at the infrastructure. Crumbled concrete and other debris littered the ground. As though he had an internal alarm clock inside his head, the *unteroffizier* awakened at the same time every morning. Nearly an entire lifetime of military training and war had produced a subconscious routine. Much like him, the warrior's comrades slowly rolled out of their bunks, preparing themselves for the beginning of another day of battle.

The *unteroffizier* slipped on his fatigues, which quite insistently proclaimed the power of the Third Reich. A soaring eagle had been stamped across the side of his helmet, its talons clasping a swastika. Iron crosses and more swastikas dangled from his uniform. For this soldier, the insignias represented power and right, at the same time that they instilled fear into the hearts of many. After holstering his sidearm, a Luger, and grabbing his helmet, the *unteroffizier* sternly walked the aisle of his barracks. His stocky shoulders were pulled back tight, and his expressionless face stared dead ahead. His skin was firm and pale. Dirt-encrusted wrinkles stretched out from his blue eyes. His pores were filled with grease and grime.

The barracks was dim due to windows long ago boarded up to mask the light from within. A series of twenty-watt light bulbs hanging over the central walkway was the main illumination, though thin cracks throughout the walls of the barracks allowed slices of sunlight to pierce through. The incandescent bulbs flickered from damp and exposed wiring. The lights reflected downward off pieces of sheet metal, revealing shadowed soldiers who looked very similar to the German *unteroffizier*, minus a large scar that reached from his right ear to his neck, just shy of his jugular. Through the speckled daylight and strobe lights overhead, the other men gathered their uniforms and equipment for the day.

Opening the door to his barracks, the *unteroffizier* exited his dim, musty quarters into a blinding wall of white sunlight. His pupils only needed a few seconds to shrink and adjust. In the distant south, he spotted large, dreary clouds moving across the sky, with strokes of gray connecting the dark blankets of moisture to the saturated earth below. Soldiers marched toward their stations, relieving antiaircraft gunners, radar monitors and maintenance men of their nightshift duties. Engineers and maintenance crews scurried around with tools and equipment. Vehicles rumbled by, carrying ammunition and aircraft parts. *Luftwaffe* fighter pilots stood out on the tarmacs, visually checking their fighter-bombers, constantly on the ready to take off at a moment's notice to defend the important installations.

Alarms suddenly began to blare just as the *unteroffizier* went for his rationed breakfast of dried eggs, bread and water, alerting the Germans of an imminent enemy assault. Memmingen's advanced radar had picked up a group of aircraft coming over the Alps, and the group's heading and location potentially threatened the aerodrome.

Before the scarred German had time to think, a senior officer was barking orders in his ear. He was to search the nearby rural lands of southern Germany and uncover downed American airmen. If any captured men tried to resist, they should be shot; otherwise, they were to be taken in for interrogation.

Two civilian bicycles commandeered a few days earlier were strapped onto a compact, four-man *Volkswagen Kübelwagen*. One bicycle was roped over the car's spare tire on the downward-slanted hood, and the other was tied down over the retracted canvas convertible top at the trunk. The *unteroffizier*, along with three other Nazis, drove out of the base's gates as the warning sirens resonated throughout the valley. If and when the Nazis saw airmen bail out, they would split up, the jeep traveling along the highways and the two bicycles traveling down country dirt roads and wooded paths. They designated a rendezvous point where they would regroup after their search.

The four soldiers rode off into the hills of their homeland.

That same morning, four United States Army Air Force officers walked the tarmac toward their B-17 bomber stationed at Sterparone Airfield, Italy. Navigator Lieutenant David Stein, co-pilot Lieutenant Harvey Myers and bombardier Lieutenant Daniel LaHurd accompanied the aircraft's pilot, Lieutenant Matthew Smith. The gunners of the airship had arrived an hour earlier and were already inside the bomber cleaning and checking their powerful .50-caliber machine guns. A team of extremely loyal and qualified men, members of the ground crew made final adjustments and checks to the B-17.

A charming extrovert from Akron, Ohio, LaHurd was twenty-five years old, six feet tall and lean. He had dark olive skin and perfectly combed black hair. His thick mustache covered his upper lip and swooped out like wings, ending in small upward twists at both ends. Only recently had dark circles begun to surround his bloodshot eyes, direct results of tense missions and tormenting nightmares that kept him tossing and turning throughout the nights. His dashing charisma and quick personality made him well liked in the bombardment group. He was a man of clear priorities: make it back to the States alive, write his family daily, take care of his comrades and, when all that was taken care of, enjoy life a little by gambling.

Smith patted LaHurd on the back as if to say, "Let's get this show on the road," and the pilot began to walk around the massive bomber, scrutinizing it with his keen and circumspect eye. Just under the pilot's window, a beautiful, blonde-haired woman with long, smooth legs had been painted across the dull aluminum surface. The words that acted as her lounge chair designated the aircraft as *Virgil's Virgins*.

The four officers' morning had started at 3:00 a.m. with a hurried breakfast and a truck ride to a secured briefing room. Hundreds of airmen, all with their own critical responsibilities, had sat on makeshift wooden benches awaiting their orders from the group's commander. LaHurd had sat between Smith and Stein. Myers had found a seat just to the left of the pilot. LaHurd and Smith had chatted about potential targets. Was it Austria, Czechoslovakia, France, Germany, Greece, Hungary, Italy, Romania, Poland or Yugoslavia? Military Police stood guard outside the only doors into the room. Each man shared the same anxieties about the day ahead. Most prayed that the mission would be a milk-run.[*]

An officer pulled two large curtains to the side, revealing a map of southern Germany. Next to the map, standing on a raised platform, the lead commander started his speech on the day's critical target: Memmingen Aerodrome. With a pointer stick in hand, he informed the men of the mission details: "The weather will be manageable. Memmingen Aerodrome activity has increased, with recent recon showing seventy to seventy-three Me 110s and Me 410s not well dispersed on the tarmacs. These double-engine fighter-bombers have a top speed of over 350 miles per hour. It's better to hit them while they are on the ground than fight them when they are shooting at us in the sky or dropping their bombs on our men. These installations are being used for repair and assembly of the planes stationed at the aerodrome. This makes Memmingen one of the highest priority counter-air targets so far in this war."

Because Memmingen was critical to the success of the *Luftwaffe*, it would be heavily defended by fighters and the unavoidable, always feared flak.[†] The

---

[*] A milk-run is slang for an easy mission.
[†] Flak is an acronym for the German phrase *flugabwehrkanone*, or aircraft defense cannon.

commander pointed out key targets dispersed throughout the aerodrome and laid out the group's flight formation. He touched on the most plausible locations where resistance would strike the group. After a quick pep talk, the men were dismissed by the newly announced lead pilot, West Point graduate Louis Seith.

Groups of men formed in small huddles to say a short prayer. They bowed their heads, closed their eyes and whispered to whatever god they believed in. The chaplain walked among them, resting his hand on the men's shoulders and praying with them. LaHurd had seen battle a number of times before. On each mission, when the flak had started exploding and the *Luftwaffe* fighters started to attack, the pact he made with his Catholic God was short and sweet: *Get me out of this mess and I promise I'll be a good man. I promise I'll do right.*

In these preflight prayers, he had time for more eloquence. He always prayed that he would see his wife, mother and father again. He prayed that his crew would be okay and complete each of their jobs with perfection and that each man would live another day. After making the sign of the cross, LaHurd and the clusters of prayers dispersed and filed out the door. From here, they marched to other briefing rooms for information unique to their crew position responsibilities and critical to the mission. Again, prayers and pep talks concluded the sessions, and the airmen marched off to gather their supplies.

Throughout the night, *Virgil's Virgins* had been equipped with thousands of rounds of ammunition for its thirteen .50-caliber machine guns, almost three thousand gallons of fuel, twelve five-hundred-pound fragmentation bombs and multiple tanks of oxygen for breathing during high-altitude flight. The ground crew specifically responsible for this B-17 made sure that they had checked every gauge, tube, rivet, control and lever on the bomber.

Best known for its daylight strategic bombing, the B-17 had a nickname through the Second World War: Flying Fortress. Nineteen feet high, 74 feet long and with a wing span of 104 feet, three of these bombers would barely fit wing to wing on a football field. The B-17 fully loaded weighed more than fifty-four thousand pounds.[*]

LaHurd and the other three officers pulled themselves up into the bottom hatch at the front of the Fortress with their cumbersome flight bags, parachute packs, oxygen masks and .45-caliber automatic handguns. Each

---

[*] The B-17 weighed approximately 36,135 pounds empty, and its maximum takeoff weight was approximately 54,000 pounds.

crew member bulked up on clothing to shield himself from the frigid, arctic-like air at high altitudes: long johns and sometimes electric underwear that connected to the aircraft's electrical system; wool pants and a wool shirt; flying coveralls; brown wool-lined jacket, hat, boots and gloves; and goggles. When the bomber reached altitudes of twenty thousand feet, the men could freeze to death within minutes if they were without such clothing. Deadly shrapnel and *Luftwaffe* fighters weren't the only hazards. Frostbite afflicted countless American airmen's limbs. Oxygen deprivation silently killed thousands of airmen. Imminent death was everywhere.

The crew of *Virgil's Virgins* would soon battle these elements together. Lieutenant Smith and his officers were partnered up with a new group of sergeants that would man the guns. Their original gunners had been assigned to a last-minute mission the afternoon before and had been given the day off. This was also Myers and Stein's first mission with the newly promoted pilot.

The interior of *Virgil's Virgins* was filled with the pungent smells of the air war: odors of fuel and oil, grease, cordite and metal. Thick tobacco smoke, potentially the airmen's last cigarette before death, filled the interior of the ribbed and riveted bomber. LaHurd's oxygen mask hung from a clip on his flight cap while he puffed away, filling his pod with smoke. One by one, the enormous bomber's four Wright Cyclone 1,400-horsepower engines rumbled to life, engulfing the plane in earthquake-like vibrations and stentorian rumbles. *Virgil's Virgins'* wheels began to roll, and the bomber taxied toward the runway, finding its place in line between the other monster birds that would soon wreak havoc over Germany.

As LaHurd's body shook from the vibrations of the bomber that housed him, he pulled an ace of spades playing card from his pocket and wedged it into a crease of his bombsight. He never left Sterparone without his good luck piece. He hoped that his superstitions would work for him and his crew members. It had so far. He thought to himself, *Mission number twenty-five, coming up. Here we go again. God be with us.*

Two bright green flares were lit off to the right of the runway, and the line of enormous bombers successively started to rumble down the sheet metal runway. *Virgil's Virgins* turned to face the airstrip, and immediately after the bomber in front became airborne, Lieutenant Smith pushed the engines to full throttle and released the brakes. His B-17 roared forward, laboring to leave the earth. At 110 miles per hour, the rubber tires of the Fortress reluctantly left the ground; the plane was airborne. It joined other bombers over Sterparone waiting for the rest of the B-17s to take off.

The Fortresses slowly assembled into their designated position over the Adriatic Sea, with more bombers from other airfields joining in. The massive war birds leveled off at approximately twenty thousand feet heading for Trieste, Italy. *Virgil's Virgins* was accompanied by B-17s from the 483rd Bombardment Group consisting of the 815th, 816th, 817th and 840th squadrons.* The bombers drew closer to one another like flocks of geese. The tight combat box allowed the group to form a cohesive defense against enemy fighters. Wingtip to wingtip, the individual B-17s' thirteen machine guns united, becoming a massive team consisting of hundreds of machine guns. Each unique Fortress, painted with its own symbol and name, became a critical wall of the newly formed fort miles above the ground, moving toward enemy skies.

Just below the pilot and copilot at the nose of the plane, LaHurd sat in a Plexiglas pod. His mouth, nose and cheeks were now covered by his oxygen mask. His goggles fit snugly over his eyes. Under his flight cap and flak helmet rested his throat microphone and headset for communications.

"How's the beer doing, boys?" he asked the gunners in the back of the plane. The crew oftentimes snuck warm beer cans onto the plane wherever they could find room, in between oxygen tanks and ammo boxes or under seats. The frigid temperatures at twenty thousand feet would freeze the liquid, giving the crew a cold celebration drink when they made it back to base with their lives.

The guts of LaHurd's bombardier pod, the real piece of equipment that got the job done, was the top-secret Norden Bombsight. Named after its inventor, Carl Norden, the sight identified targets and aimed bombs with more precision than ever before. A small telescope containing two cross hairs—one to show drift left or right of the targets and the other to show rate of closure—allowed LaHurd to more accurately aim his bombs.

Over the Adriatic Sea, the ball turret gunner lowered his Plexiglas pod, squeezed himself inside and fired a short burst from his .50- caliber guns. The other gunners followed suit. Quick bursts of fire shook the bomber. Gunners throughout the formation joined in. The sky cracked as the strapping guns cleared their throats. With the gunners satisfied that their weapons were in top order, they sat back and scanned the open stretch of blue and white, searching for enemy fighters. The assemblage of bombers rumbled toward a white wall of cumulus clouds high above the shores of the Adriatic. As fifty-

---

* A bombardment group usually had four squadrons. Each squadron had eight to twelve bombers.

degree-below-zero winds rushed over the aluminum riveted bomber at its cruising speed of 180 miles per hour, the panoply of black dots that littered the sky entered a bank of thick clouds.

Minus the fear and constant thought of death, the freezing cold was the worst part of the mission for most of the crew. LaHurd had always hated the cold. The winters back home, the snow, the ice, the chilly wind, had never been his favorite. The temperatures up here were bone chilling. The subzero air seemed to pass right through every layer of clothing that covered his body, right through his skin, freezing his bones and blood. His shivering hands, protected under thick gloves, struggled to control his bombsight's dials. Small ice crystals formed around his oxygen mask where condensation from breathing built up.

While the Fortress pushed through the clouds, LaHurd studied maps and pictures of the targets he would soon pummel with the five-hundred-pound bombs waiting in the belly of the bomber. His mind drifted between his task at hand and his family and wife. Fifty was the magic number. LaHurd would be homebound if he could reach fifty successful missions. The army air forces had promised the men that much, giving the airmen more reason to risk their lives and face the insurmountable odds stacked against them. Homebound meant that Daniel could travel the five thousand miles to his family and wife in Akron, Ohio.

Due to the blinding expanse of mystifying white, the men had zero visibility, and the symmetry of the group's box formation was dangerously dispersed throughout the sky. Flight formations were made impossible by the invisible line of travel. The possibility of aircrafts smashing into one another was highly probable. Unable to maneuver through the inhospitable weather, forty-four B-17s returned to base, while another twenty-seven attacked an alternate target. The aerial fort was losing its strength brick by brick. As the number of bombers decreased, the fortification of the formation was less likely to hold up.

The remaining bombers moved forward to the rendezvous point at Trieste to meet up with the American fighter escort and carry on with the mission. Unfortunately, bad weather upset the schedule, and that rendezvous never happened. These courageous airmen moved forward to accomplish the bombing run unescorted by their protectors. It was now up to the individual gunner to defend his ship.

As LaHurd watched his odds of getting back to Sterparone Airfield diminish, he and the remaining members of the 483rd Bombardment Group continued on with their next leg over the frigid Alps to the valley city of

Innsbruck, Austria. From Innsbruck, the remaining bombers headed into southwestern Germany to Kempten, where their initial point of the bombing run began for the Memmingen Aerodrome.

At 450 miles into the mission, the crew broke through the clouds to a newly visible world. The sky was blue and the land below was peaceful and calm. From this altitude, Earth seemed utterly serene, as if it were moving in slow motion. Small villages dotted the land on the foothills of the Alps. The view of snow-capped mountains gradually transformed into forested hills and then to an endless sea of verdant green patches of farmland.

The placid scene was short-lived. The clouds had parted at the wrong moment. The bombers were no longer under cover, and at the group's three o'clock position, what looked like a scattering of numerous little black dots moved in the opposite direction. Hearts began to pound as adrenaline pumped through the airmen. Gunners, covered in heavily reinforced metal flak vests, with faces hidden behind large goggles, looked like extraterrestrials as they clenched their .50-caliber machine guns, preparing for the inevitable fighter assault.

German Me 109s and Fw 190s maneuvered for a tail attack. Seventy-five elusive and agile fighters with a top speed of over 320 miles per hour pursued twenty-six lumbering heavy bombers loaded with tons of bombs crawling across the sky. Without a single American fighter plane to protect them, the odds that this group would be exterminated seemed overwhelmingly high. The determination of the crews eliminated the option of aborting. As the enemy fighters moved in for the kill, another force, even larger than the first, dropped in behind the initial wave.

Over two hundred enemy fighters leveled off. They came in close and fired on the rear position of the bomber group as the phalanx of Fortresses passed over small quaint villages. Enemy cannons began to flash like strings of blinking Christmas lights. Bullets and tracers littered the skies as the German fighters started to assault the bombers. Two Fortresses began to billow thick black smoke into the atmosphere as they fragmented.

The hearts of the *Virgil's Virgins* gunners thumped so hard they thought they would blow out of their chests. They had been in this situation before, but it never became routine. Their sweaty hands under thick gloves clasped their .50-caliber machine guns. Within minutes, the seven hapless B-17s belonging to the 816th Squadron in the back of the formation were spinning helplessly toward the ground while gunners still held their positions and fired toward the crescendo of attacking fighters. Some never made it out of their bomber before crashing, disintegrating and making a cratered grave.

As bullets whizzed through the air, the next wave of the *Luftwaffe* attack concentrated its fire on the 817th Squadron. Horace Davenport, crammed tightly into the rear of *Virgil's Virgins*, communicated to the rest of the crew through a crackling microphone. He had an unimpeded view of the fighter assault through his tail gun's Plexiglas window. The bomber's four engines droning through the air made it difficult to hear, and as soon as the massive guns began to fire, communication would become almost impossible.

"There's a shitload of fighters coming up fast on our six," howled Davenport through the microphone system.

He made the sign of the cross and watched the slaughter of the 816th Squadron. He counted the parachutes as the crewmen bailed from their planes into the blue sky. The buzzing fighters neared *Virgil's Virgins*, and Davenport squeezed the trigger of his machine gun. The plane shook and thumped from the recoil of the powerful gun. Tracers streamed from the rear of the Fortress.

The ball turret gunner, Carl E. May, hanging vulnerably from the bottom of the bomber in a Plexiglas semi-globe, hollered through the communication system, "I got three 109s coming from below."

His pod swiveled slightly to the right, and his .50-calibers sprayed a deadly barrage of lead into the air. May had managed to clip one Me 109 with his storm of bullets. A contrail of smoke stretched from the fighter's engine into the sky as it spun away from the bomber. The other two fighters made a break up and to the right, exposing their bellies to John E. Papamanoli, manning another .50-caliber at the right waist of the aircraft. His gun began to pump and shake as he clutched his trigger. Just behind him stood William M. Marlin, defending the opposite side of *Virgil's Virgins*. Marlin's gun pumped away at a pair of fighters approaching from up and to the left of his position. Out of the corner of his eye, he saw a fellow B-17's engine begin to puff gray smoke, quickly followed by thick black smoke. Another engine on the right wing followed suit. The bomber dropped down and to the right, out of his sight. He silently asked God to be with his falling comrades.

Spent shells the length of a man's hand began to fill the floor of the riveted interior of the Fortress. The crosswind of the gunners' open windows froze the interior of the bomber; ice covered the floor and riveted walls. Empty shells were scattered across the walkway, smoking and steaming. The interior began to fill with the stinging smell of cordite from exploding gunpowder exhausted from the .50-caliber guns. The scent was nearly suffocating. Endless smoke bursts and tiny flames cracked from the defensive weapons within the Flying Fortress. Clouds of oil and soot clogged the air and clung to the airmen's clothing, skin and goggles. Gunners' breaths grew heavy from high adrenaline. Their goggles fogged, and the condensation instantly froze. They frantically scraped at the frost and soot over their goggles to regain sight. Searching the skies through scratches of frost, the gunners bravely defended their aerial fort.

Lloyd Venables, the engineer, responsible for looking over the pilot's and copilot's shoulders and monitoring all gauges and dials, was stationed at his top turret gun, his monitoring duties pushed aside. At this moment, he was more concerned with protecting the bomber. From his elevated position, he could see the flock of fighters throughout the sky zipping around with great speed. Marlin's bullets caused the two fighters in his sights to pull up and break away from the bomber. As soon as they gained altitude, Venables's top turret gun, synchronized so that it could not fire when it came in line with the tail of his aircraft, came to life. The *Luftwaffe* pilots twisted and turned their fighters unsuccessfully in their attempts to avoid the maelstrom of deadly metal. Almost instantly, both fighters' right wings turned to debris and spun off into the sky like leaves on a stormy autumn day. The remaining body and left wing of each fighter tumbled through the air uncontrollably.

Venables's scream, slightly diffused by static, crackled through the mike as he watched the fighters spin to earth, "Go to hell, you Kraut bastards!"

A lone fighter made a pass at a bomber flying just off the right wing of *Virgil's Virgins*. His cannons flickered, sending out a deadly stream of fire that ripped through the bomber's tail and belly. Debris fell from the Fortress, making a number of gaping holes the size of footballs. *Virgil's Virgins* Radio Operator Ackley Doverspike and the gunners of the targeted bomber fired at the fighter plane. The fighter was caught in the crossfire. The *Luftwaffe* pilot tilted his wing and dropped down and out of the predicament, only to travel into the territory of both bombers' ball turret gunners, who simultaneously swiveled into position and pulled their triggers, aiming just ahead of the fleeing fighter. The blessed *Luftwaffe* pilot managed to avoid all the shots aimed his way. He dropped back and readied his aircraft for another pass.

Just underneath the pilot and copilot and behind the bombardier, David Stein, the navigator, sat surrounded by windows. A Plexiglas dome used for celestial navigation bulged from the ceiling. Machine guns jutted out from each side of his station. He multitasked among navigating the plane, communicating the bomber's headings to the pilot and firing bursts from either of his two guns.

Matthew Smith, the pilot, and Harvey Meyers, the copilot, sat in their heated compartment trying to maintain a straight heading to avoid the other bombers in the formation. Midair collisions had accounted for countless wrecks and bailouts, and Smith was conscious not to let that happen to his plane. There was a lot going on, but the mission was to get to the target, and Smith had every intention of doing so. The pilot used all of his muscle to keep the bomber steady and on course so LaHurd could perform the necessary calculations of drift, altitude and speed for his bombing run.

Just outside the target, Smith placed the bomber on autopilot and handed over the flying to the bombardier. LaHurd controlled the plane with his Norden Bombsight. As he adjusted his scope, the plane slightly altered course to accommodate.

LaHurd was also responsible for manning the twin .50-caliber guns at the chin of the plane. If a fighter decided to make a head-on attack at the Fortress, LaHurd and Venables would be the defense. Until "Bombs Away" was heard over the microphone, LaHurd was in full command. He was in control of the bombs, and at this instant, he was one of the most dangerous men in the world. The target was only twenty miles away.

Mission number fifty grew further and further from LaHurd's mind as he realized from the tracers traveling past his window that the attacking foes were concentrating their firepower on his plane. The aluminum exterior of the Flying Fortress was no match for the cannon fire ripping through its skin. Shrapnel splintered through the interior of the aircraft. The soft metal peeled away like a banana. The gunners were doing all they could to defend their Fortress, but there were just too many fighters. Suddenly, 30mm cannons tore through the tail of the bomber. Davenport's gunner pod looked as though it had been run through a meat grinder. The shredded tail looked like a splintered tree branch. Pieces of bent and split metal jutted out into the sky. Davenport's brain never even had enough time to register pain before the cannon fire blew through his body, killing him instantly.

As in all the other times LaHurd had found himself in this situation, he began to pray: *Dear God, please get me out of this mess. I swear I'll be a good man. No more alcohol, no more gambling, no more cigarettes.*

The body and wings of the Flying Fortress could handle a high degree of destruction. Oftentimes, these bombers returned to base with missing noses, thousands of cannon holes, severed wingtips or gaping wounds the size of Volkswagens. But the Nazis' firepower finally took its toll on the bomber as the enemy's cannons tore through the two engines on *Virgil's Virgins'* right wing. The plane began to billow thick black smoke and fire. The engines

B-17F Flying Fortress.

rattled and shook. Debris and flames from the mangled engines chewed away at the right wing of the bomber until half of it finally broke loose and flipped away from the aircraft. The B-17 rapidly lost stability and began its final, uncontrolled descent toward the ground.

LaHurd became disoriented as smoke filled the aircraft. The massive bomber was no more than a disintegrating chunk of metal.

"Get out! Get out now!" ordered Smith over the mike as he activated the bailout light.

Molten metal fell from the sky like rain. The last thing any man wanted to do was jump from a burning bomber out into a sky of burning debris and bullets to slowly descend onto Nazi land. But after the pilot gave a final order, the men had little choice.

LaHurd and Stein squeezed through the smoke-filled nose and scurried over molten .50-caliber shells toward the exit hatch on the floor. They needed to survive, and that meant they needed to jump out of the hurling piece of wreckage. Just before LaHurd pulled the emergency release handle of the forward door near the nose of the plane to bail out, he looked up to see Smith and Myers climbing down toward the hatch. The men clipped their parachutes onto their harnesses, double-checked the clips, triple-checked the clips, kicked open the frozen door, made the sign of the cross and began to jump out into the freezing stratosphere one by one.

Chapter 2

BOUNCING BETTY

March 13, 1942–June 23, 1942

*I fear all we have done is awaken a sleeping giant
and fill him with a terrible resolve.*
—*Isoroku Yamamoto*

On the military transportation train, the third cabin back from the engine, Private Daniel Elias LaHurd shared a row with his longtime friend Private Tony Testa. He and Tony had enlisted together to avenge the Japanese attacks on Pearl Harbor only four months earlier. American patriotism and instant antipathy toward Japan had filled recruitment lines in every state. Aside from the desire for retribution, everyone else was enlisting, so why not him? It would be an adventure.

The troop train seemed to stretch for miles. Coaches, flatbeds loaded with war material, kitchen cars and baggage cars were linked together for the long journey. Throughout the war, these troop trains were a key part of the war effort and carried all kinds of cargo, from the president and his generals to migrant farmers, weapons to mail, food and even Axis prisoners of war.

Pressurized steam hissed out from beneath the engine over a grid of steel tracks and railroad ties. As the depot slowly rolled past LaHurd's window, men in top hats and trench coats, predominantly fathers and brothers of the departing soldiers, waved goodbye. Mothers, sisters and wives, dressed primly for the gravity of the occasion, beckoned with handkerchiefs in hand as their eyes swelled with tears. Children raced alongside the train, flapping tiny American flags in the chilled air.

Groups of excited soldiers huddled around open windows to catch sight of their families for one last time. A number of the riders dangled their upper bodies out of the cabin's windows, blowing kisses to loved ones through the cold air. LaHurd caught a glimpse of his own family huddled close to one another with smiles on their faces and energetic waves goodbye. Tony's family stood by the LaHurds, keeping one another company as their two boys moved away from the concrete platform of the depot.

Tony and Daniel had the same thought: *I hope nothing happens to me. I sure want to see these good people again.* LaHurd watched his family grow smaller and disappear. His new life had just begun.

At twenty-three years old, Daniel was considered a mature enlistee who, only a few months prior, had been working in his father's grocery stores and living a relatively secluded lifestyle. After he graduated high school, he played a few years of football, tailback, at Kent State University. There, he studied business until he recognized that college wasn't his destiny and professors were not easily charmed. Work, cards, family and the local nightlife had made up Daniel's life. As he surveyed the cabin, his maturity showed. A number of the more juvenile boys, some seventeen and eighteen years old, looked like kids.

The thin window curtains did little to mask the setting sun. The greenhouse effect kept the car warm and clammy, creating a musty smell. The low hum of GI chatter provided a constant monotonous murmur. LaHurd's window, only about the size of a propaganda poster, would serve as a stage to the diverse landscape of the vast countryside outside. Palm trees, deserts, mountains, forests, big cities would bring new perspective to this Akron, Ohio native who had rarely left his hometown.

Daniel and Tony added to the chatter, their voices muffled by the sound of the rumbling steel wheels against metal tracks. The troop train cleared Port Clinton and the Sandusky, Ohio area around 5:30 p.m., steaming for Chicago. As the train turned slightly north, the sun made its final appearance just above the horizon.

The sky was beautiful. A brilliant mosaic of oranges and reds painted the heavens. Dispersed pink clouds hung motionless in the evening sky. Looking out to the horizon as his train pushed across the farmlands of northwestern Ohio, LaHurd's view to the west was hampered only by the curving earth. The stretch of flat land seemed to go on forever. Across the aisle, out the opposite window, the eastern sky was dark. Wheat stocks outside his window, hugging the train's tracks, passed by in a blur. The train gradually snaked left as it headed west, chasing the setting sun.

LaHurd was on his way to cities and lands he'd only read about in magazines and newspapers. His life from this point on was yet to be written. Daily routine and the safe familiarity of his hometown were in the past, in the dark east, in the opposite direction of where he was heading. For all his excitement, he was a little afraid, although he would never admit it to the fellows sitting around him, not even Tony.

After a few hours, the train's friction against the rails became monotonous and somewhat rhythmic. LaHurd's eyes grew heavy. To his right, Tony was asleep. The enthusiasm and chatter had subsided. Body heat from the draftees kept the interior warm. The sun had completely disappeared. Exhausted from the turbulent emotions of parting with his family and the mixture of anxiety and excitement for his new adventure, LaHurd's eyes surrendered to the weight of his eyelids.

The train, quickly coined the *Bouncing Betty* by the young men in LaHurd's cabin, began to slow, blowing its whistle to alert passengers that they had reached their first destination: Chicago. At 9:30 p.m., the train completed its slow deceleration at a depot just southwest of the downtown area. Due to the commotion of the slowing locomotive and his fellow cadets' exclamations, LaHurd awakened. Only a short time earlier, his window had been filled with hopeful families and endless farmland. Now, he was looking out on a bustling city filled with luminous skyscrapers and throngs of people. Akron was nothing like this. Thirty to forty more men entered *Bouncing Betty* and got situated among the others already on board, and the train resumed its clamorous ride.

The next morning, the troop train pulled into Kansas City. Here, the cadets were given enough time to depart the depot and get breakfast on Uncle Sam's tab. Their allowance was five dollars a day, a sufficient amount for meals. After a quick breakfast of ham, eggs and toast, *Bouncing Betty* was off again with more troops and more equipment.

Two days after leaving Port Clinton, LaHurd sent a postcard home from his next stop, Belen, New Mexico: "We stopped in this little western town, and I saw a few Indians. This train rocks more than a battleship but I'm getting used to it." When he crossed the southern border of California, he wrote home, "Crossed into California last night about 10:00 p.m. We passed Santa Anita Race track this morning and what little I saw of it was beautiful. Calif. is really beautiful. I saw palm trees, orange trees, and mountains."

His training would soon begin. His desire to vindicate America and confront its infamous attacker would soon be within reach. Only one month before Daniel's train departed from Port Clinton, he had informed his family that he had enlisted in the United States Army Air Force.

It was a Sunday afternoon in February. Like every Sunday, the family met at Daniel's parents' home in Akron. The city had become one of the fastest-growing areas in the country during the 1920s and '30s. The manufacturing of rubber tires had created an explosion of employment opportunities inside the factories there. Migrant workers from neighboring states and European immigrants had raced into the area to work for one of the four big companies of tire production: Goodyear, Goodrich, General and Firestone. Akron had quickly transformed from a small canal town of the 1850s into a burgeoning industrial city.

During the war, Akron produced two-thirds of all heavy tires needed for military guns and supply trucks and one-half of all U.S. heavy-duty tires. The huge output made the Akron air thick with stinging odors of burnt rubber. The majority of Akron's citizens literally lived and breathed rubber, helping the world nickname the city the "Rubber Capital of the World."

Within the Rubber Capital sat the LaHurd residence at 1099 Berwin Street. The red brick road was lined with huge oak and cherry trees that created a canopy over the neighborhood. Up and down the quiet street, flags hanging in house windows and painted across sheds displayed a persistent American patriotism. Like a light switch, the tragic attacks on Pearl Harbor had instantly turned off pre-attack isolationism and ignited a steely determination within most local communities.

The LaHurd home, a sizeable two-story house, had a large front porch where much of the summer and fall months were spent drinking tea and chatting with friends and family. Daniel's mother, Mary, a quiet woman, was kind and loving. Her husband, Joseph, known to the family as Pa Joe, was a well-manicured, intelligent businessman. As the general manager of Square Deal Grocery Stores, he had provided a good living through the depressed years of the 1930s and produced a comfortable life for his wife and five children. Louise was twenty-seven, the oldest child in the LaHurd clan. She was a gentle, kindhearted and caring mother for her two daughters, Linda Lou and Mary Lou. She had married the man of her dreams, Alan, a star football player and gregarious gentleman. Michael, two years younger than his sister, had the appearance of a born soldier: compact and stocky. His chest was wide and defined, arms ripped with muscle and calves hard as bricks. His wife, Beulah, thought by many to be the sweetest woman in town, watched over her son Neil. Fred, nineteen, was quiet in comparison to his brothers. His body was much like Michael's, with a thick neck and gruff face that resembled a boxer, though through and through Fred was an engaging and respectful man. Calvin, tall and slender, was the youngest at seventeen. He reminded many people around town of his father. He was clean cut and respectful. His bushy black eyebrows stood out from his defined face and soft cheekbones. Daniel called him "the Babe" because of his boyish good looks. His sporadic comedic comments were hilarious surprises for many.

As Catholics, the family went to church together every Sunday and looked forward to the meal that awaited them on those evenings.

Outside, small snowflakes fell from the sky on the wintry February Sunday. The sun had disappeared beneath the horizon, creating a drastic temperature drop. The streetcars, operating on the road perpendicular to Berwin Street, were temporarily shut down due to the deep snow that had fallen throughout the day. Occasional gusts of bone-chilling wind howled around the house, making the family appreciative of the warm fireplace within.

Mary prepared the table with the usual Lebanese favorites. Intermingled odors of lemon, cinnamon, onion, garlic and parsley permeated the air as plates of kibbeh naye, wara' enab, hummus and tabouleh were crammed onto the dining room table. After Pa Joe whispered a short prayer, dishes began to clang as spoons and knives dug into the exotic foods. The mood was cheery, and the pleasant bonhomie was incomparable to anywhere else. Brother and sister told stories of the previous week's activities, joked with one another and stuffed their mouths with delicious food. Small talk about the war was the locus of conversation. In the adjacent room, Pa Joe and Mary's grandchildren sat at a small table, where they gorged themselves with food. The radio, sitting next to the burning fireplace, played current favorites.

After the LaHurds had finished dinner, coffee was served. If any time was right, Daniel knew this was it. He stood, a healthy young man greatly adored by his entire family, tapped his glass with a fork that still held small crumbs of tabouleh and said, "As you all know, the thought that I must do something for this country in the time of war has been nagging at me." He spoke as if he had recited this speech over and over again in preparation.

Daniel continued, "Tony and I went to the recruiting station and signed up for the army air force. If possible, I want to be a pilot; if not, I will contribute in whatever way I can. My training should start in March. I hope that you all will accept my decision."

He immediately sat back down, relieved that the news was out. He waited for the lecture from his father. It never came. Mary's and Louise's eyes swelled with tears. Pa Joe stood, raised his glass and made a toast wishing his son good luck. His brother Mike patted Beulah's shoulder while he shook his head with concern for his younger brother. Calvin and Fred stood, raised their glasses and made a toast wishing Daniel luck. Nothing else was said by his family that evening about the war or the fact that their brother and son would soon be fighting in it. An unusual silence fell across the table—a silence that would become commonplace in the years to come.

Lurching forward, the train's wheels made their final turn, concluding the three-and-a-half-day, two-thousand-plus mile journey across the country. Just beyond the depot sat one of the largest training classification centers in the world. Cadets from all over the United States, young men striving to become pilots, navigators, engineers and bombardiers, walked through the same entrance into the colossal training camp located just thirty miles from Los Angeles, California.

Santa Ana Army Air Base (SAAAB) stretched out over 1,400 acres of Southern Californian landscape. The camp had the capacity to house over 26,000 men. The barracks, tents, hospital wards, schools, chapels, theaters and administrative buildings covered more land than six U.S. Pentagons placed side by side, just over 1.35 million square feet. This classification and pre-flight training camp pumped out nearly 129,000 graduates through the course of World War II. Thousands more passed through its gates as redistributed combatants, temporary residents, veteran discharges, Japanese aliens awaiting transportation to their homeland and German POWs.

The moment that Daniel stepped off the train, his way of life would be altered in every way. His clothing, posture, diet, exercise, sleeping habits and bathroom habits, not to mention his skills in organization, communication and leadership, would all be closely monitored and tweaked to fit that of a disciplined American airman.

LaHurd was assigned to Company 24 and shown the tent that he would briefly call home. Throughout his three-month stay at SAAAB, he switched from tent to barracks and from barracks to tent so many times that at the end of a long and stressful day, he was often confused as to where his bunk was actually located. From Company 24, Daniel moved to Company 26, then Company 17, then Company 27 and then back to Company 24. With each change, he was forced to move his living quarters, packing his belongings, uprooting, unpacking and resettling. It was a frustrating and annoying cycle. He wrote home, "I move around as much here that I never know what Company I'll be in the next day." He preferred, as most of the other cadets, barracks over tents. Each room within the barracks housed six men and kept them comfortably sheltered from the outdoor elements.

Daniel's first month on base was filled with preparatory tasks and assignments. Before all else, he needed the appropriate equipment and appearance. LaHurd was given two monkey suits—flight suits—and received an old-fashioned army haircut. He was also given a rifle to carry while marching, the first gun he had ever held. Best of all, he was issued his first military uniform. LaHurd wrote to his father, "Boy are our uniforms nice, we look like a million bucks in them."

His mornings at SAAAB were rough at first and differed significantly from his accustomed routine back in Akron. Each day started before sunrise with his vigorous lieutenant barging into the cadets' quarters, hollering and screaming for the men to "drop your cocks, and get up ladies." Daniel and his tent mates shaved, cleaned themselves up and had the tent in order for inspection by 6:00 a.m. Following inspection, they were exercised for thirty minutes, fed breakfast and lined up on the parade field to practice marching.

The parade field was filled with embryonic airmen from all across the country. Most of these men had zero military training. They had worked in their local communities as butchers, salesmen, steelworkers, coal miners, barbers, mechanics or farmers. Some were fresh out of high school, and some hadn't even made it to their senior year. Most had one goal in mind— to fly, or at least become airborne. The training and expectations were tough, some thought absurdly unfeasible. Marching was one elemental way to bond a disparate group of individuals into a disciplined unit. Their first few attempts at becoming a suitable group was a blunder, as LaHurd described to his parents in a letter home: "This morning we went out to the field to practice marching and what a sorry looking bunch we made but at least I'm getting a suntan."

Slightly more than 50 percent of these untaught cadets eventually failed either the initial physical or written test and were packed off to the infantry. Nearly 40 percent of the men who were fortunate enough to move forward with specific training schools eventually washed out. The cadets' future was determined by their performance in this nine-week training camp and the weeks, sometimes months, of physical testing and schooling that they endured. Here psychologists and doctors monitored, measured and scrutinized the cadets' eyesight, mental aptitude, motor coordination and psychological stability, with the outcome eventually determining which training school they were assigned to. Each man received a multitude of shots, X-rays, blood tests and dental inspections. They were judged and graded by class participation, paper exams and physical exams on a base that was absent of planes, runways and hangars.

LaHurd's weakness was quickly recognized by the medical staff: the doctors found an imperfection in the excessive amounts of cartilage inside his nose. They feared that his constrained nasal cavities could constrict breathing at high-altitude flight. After just ten days at SAAAB, LaHurd was in the hospital, writing home.

Dear Pa,

They finally operated on my nose after being in the hospital two days doing nothing. They operated Thursday about 2:45 P.M. and finished about 3:00 P.M. so now I am able to breath through both nostrils. They took the bandages off the next day and I'll leave the hospital Mon. or Tues.

The doctor who operated was one swell fellow. During the operation he talked and kidded with me. Although they blindfolded me I still could see a little but couldn't feel nothing. I could hear the bones crack and when he used the hammer and chisel a couple times I thought he was going to take my nose off. After the operation I could hardly keep my eyes open. I was so drowsy but I feel fine today.

I received your letter and package but I haven't opened the package as yet because I want to wait till I get out of here because if it is something good to eat I'll have to pass it around so I don't want to take any chances.

XXOOOXX

Dan

The military was doing everything in its conceivable power to create perfect warriors. Any small blemish to a cadet in America could become a huge problem to that same man overseas. If Daniel was unable to obtain enough oxygen on high-altitude flights, he could pass out, consequently jeopardizing his mission and even his life.

On May 6, LaHurd was classified as pilot, and with that classification followed classes, exams and hours of studying. He'd learn code, geometry and trigonometry, plane recognition, physics, map studies and ground forces. Schooling was fast paced, detailed and difficult.

Dear Pa + Ma

We really have a stiff schedule now. We get up at 5: A.M. and have reveille at 5:30; eat at 6 A.M. come back to our barracks and clean our rooms by 6:45, fall out for classes at 6:45 and go to school till 10:30. Well after classes we come back to our barracks and take a quick smoke and then fall out for mess at 11 A.M; then from 12 to 1 P.M. we either have chemical warfare or military courtesy; from 1:30 to 2:30 we have drill; from 3 to 4 athletics; from 4:30 to 4:50 we have retreat and at 5: P.M. we have mess and after mess we're supposed to study for two hours. So you can see that our time is pretty well taken up and if we do find a little time for ourselves they are always sure to give us something to do to keep us busy.

I'm feeling swell so you don't have to worry about my health as the army doesn't give me a chance to run my health down. (knock knock) I haven't weighed myself for several weeks but you can be sure I haven't lost any weight, I probably gained a couple of pounds more.

Your letters have been coming pretty regular except when they bounce from one squadron to another. You know how they kept moving me, well even the army can't keep up with me. Pa instead of using company 27 now use Squadron 27 they're getting high class around here.

Well I went to my first code class today and learned 4 letters in code. (A) (E) (N) (T) we are supposed to learn four new letters each day and boy it is really going to be tough learning 26 letters and 10 numerals, 36 in all. Math is getting a little harder now and they really pour it to us. They say that one hour here is equal to one week in college.

Tell Lou and Mike I'll try to answer their letters as soon as I get a chance and have something interesting to write. I have to close now as I have to finish my math problems.

P.S. I don't need a thing so thanks anyhow.

Love
Dan

The cadets' studies were coupled with calisthenics, cross-country runs, mental and physical exams, Kitchen Patrol, Fire Guard and Guard Duty. LaHurd treasured Fire Guard Duty: "I got me a nice soft detail today, Fire Guard. The only thing I have to do is look for fires in our barracks and one look is enough for me so the rest of the time I can rest for my weekend." The men were exposed to first aid techniques and survival training. They received information on poisonous snakes; the edibility of wild fruits, berries, nuts and roots; and how to make shelters and keep dry in the rain—all pertinent information that could be critical to their survival in enemy territory.

Their grueling training was broken up with weekend passes and visitors from Hollywood. Because of the base's proximity to the star-studded city, many Hollywood actors frequented Santa Ana to entertain the cadets. During LaHurd's tenure, he was amazed to see stars such as Bob Hope, the ventriloquist Edgar Bergen and Charlie McCarthy, Duke Ellington, Phil Harris, Eddie Cantor and Jack Benny. Hollywood also became a recurrent weekend hangout for the freshly minted military men who needed a break from war preparations. These twenty-four-hour trips, like mail from home, were major morale boosters that kept the men going. For the first thirty days, the cadets were restricted from leaving the base, but thereafter, they were awarded weekend passes, giving them permission to leave the gates of SAAAB without supervision.

LaHurd often splurged and stayed the night at the Biltmore, one of Los Angeles's finest hotels. His current net income of seventy-five dollars per month was considerably higher than the average American's salary of thirty to forty dollars per month. He could afford to splurge occasionally. His main expenses per month were cleaning bills, laundry, rations and occasionally discretionary purchases such as a six-dollar pair of new sunglasses, comfortable shoes, a dress shirt or an eight-dollar gym outfit.

The weekends off and the nightlife really appealed to LaHurd. He had an engaging personality coupled with a mature charm, and he wasn't afraid to walk up and chat with the ladies. With his new uniform, California sun tan and (thanks to the military dentist) brilliant smile, it seemed as though the California women flocked to the Akronite. He had it all: good looks, charisma, discretionary income and a soldier's status.

Dear Folks

I received that important letter today and thanks loads, by the way how did you know I was broke. I spent my last two dollars Saturday and it was really worth it, as I had a real swell time and you see, I haven't been broke long but long enough.

You said in your letter that you haven't heard from me for several days but I been writing my daily card faithfully and I don't know what could have happened to them.

Saturday I went swimming in the Pacific and sail boating in the bay and that evening I met more women than I knew what to do with but I'll manage. I have a date with one girl at 4:30 P.M. next Sat. and she's going to pick me up in her car and I have a date with another at 9 P.M. and the third girl I'm suppose to call so you can see that I'll have my hands full. I'll be well taken care of next Sat. All that on two dollars, so you can see I did a lot of things in Long Beach on two bucks. I wrote you a card Sat. and some girl was going to mail it for me but I snuck out on her and I don't know if she'll mail it or tear it.

I weighed myself Sat. and weighed 170 with my clothes on and I don't know if the scale is wrong or I have put on that much weight and I hope the scale is right and I'll bet you do to.

We had our final today and tomorrow we find out our grades and I'll let you know how I make out.

By the way, did you receive my photos?

Pa, I want you to go to the bank and draw out twenty dollars and give Cal + Fred each ten for their high school graduation present for me and tell them to take their girls out and really have a good time. This is a business deal, you know! They'll be working soon sooo; you know!

I'm feeling swell and school is coming along. I think I'll get by. I hope everything is coming along fine for you. I mean your not pressed for money and can meet all the bills as you must have plenty of them with the rug, car and radio to pay on.

Give my best girl (Ma) a big hug and kiss for me and tell her I really appreciate her saving that money for me.

Love + Kisses

Dan

One thing that LaHurd and almost all the other cadets struggled with was Sunday parade. The cadets, out late drinking and partying with the ladies the night before, oftentimes had miserable hangovers the next day. One particular Friday, Daniel wrote home, "Tomorrow afternoon I'm going to L.A. and get good and drunk and maybe it will clear my head as they been rushing us pretty fast in school." That Sunday, another letter home described the morning after his Saturday binge: "I never should have drank that much, Sunday parade was hell."

During one of LaHurd's countless moves from company to company, he was assigned to a new barracks, and to his astonishment, Tony Testa became his roommate. LaHurd and Tony attempted to have as much fun and bend as many rules as possible before Tony was shipped out to navigation school. He had been an inch too short for piloting but was "tickled pink" about heading to navigation training.

Folks,

Tony and I got caught sleeping in the other morning and had to clean the latrine but this morning we slept till about 8:00 and got away with it while the rest of the Co. got up at 5:45. You know how I like my sleep.

Last Friday an order came out that we would get 24 passes but Sat. they said, that was only for fellows who have been at a West Coast Replacement Center for 50 days so we were a disappointed branch of fellows up till about 5:00 P.M. Sat. when the captain walked in our tent checking bed lockers. So I asked him if there was a chance to get a pass and he said what I thought he would say "NO" and so Tony tells him his wife is coming in from Ohio and that she would really be disappointed but I guess the Captain knew he was telling a lie because he looked at me and started to smile and the rest of the fellows in the tent started to laugh. So as he was leaving the tent he told us to stand by and he would have a detail for us to do and we would get passes when we finished. Our faces turned from a gloomy look to smiles. So we four fellows out of about 100 others got passes and did we razz and get razzed for kissing the Captains A...

Tell Cal + Fred to write often.

P.S. Cal + Fred you should see those P-38 fighters dive and loop around here. Boy they really go.

Love
Dan

After the successful completion of LaHurd's coursework, physical exams and mental exams, the time had come for him to ship out to primary, the first phase in becoming a pilot. He was happy about his classification and his move, as he explained to his family: "We will be pulling out for primary the first of this week and it's about time as I'm getting sick of staying so long in one place." He was excited that his last days at Santa Ana were finally upon him. Soon he would be shipped off to one of the six primary schools that were located within a one-hundred-mile radius of one another.

Primary was rumored to have better facilities, food and accommodations than SAAAB. Daniel didn't know exactly which base he would be sent to because the military held such information until the last minute to keep civilians and the enemy from knowing the logistics of troop movement.

The rumor in the latrine had been that the men would ship out within the next two days to somewhere in California. The rumor would turn out to be correct.

Before leaving SAAAB, LaHurd purchased an album for autographs and photographs. Within a few days, hundreds of signatures and witty lines filled the album's pages. Anxious cadets wrote:

> *We all have a common ambition, TOKYO!!*
> *Hirohito, here we come!*
> *We won't always be in the army. We'll either be out of it or pushing up daisies.*
> *I hope I can visit Tokyo with you Danny.*
> *You have become a swell friend. You can have anything of mine—except my wife.*

LaHurd packed up his belongings, turned in his bedding and was ready to leave for primary, where he would finally sit in an airplane and become a flyboy. His excitement was not without some anxiety. He knew the odds of being washed out were high. He had heard stories from the men who had washed out from flight training and were sent back to Santa Ana to be reclassified.

Daniel wrote home:

> *My buddy flunked out in his flying ability and not his academic studies at primary. The army wants you to fly their way and if you can't your just out and they only give you eight hours and then you solo. That doesn't seem like much to learn how to take a plane up and land it after eight hours of instructions but they [the army] thinks so....And, If I can get passed the first few hours I believe I'll be alright but I'll probably be scared silly. I'll soon find out.*

Though he doubted himself and his abilities, he figured it was worth a shot. At 6:00 p.m. on June 23, 1942, the men grabbed their bags and headed for the troop train. LaHurd was off to Visalia, California.

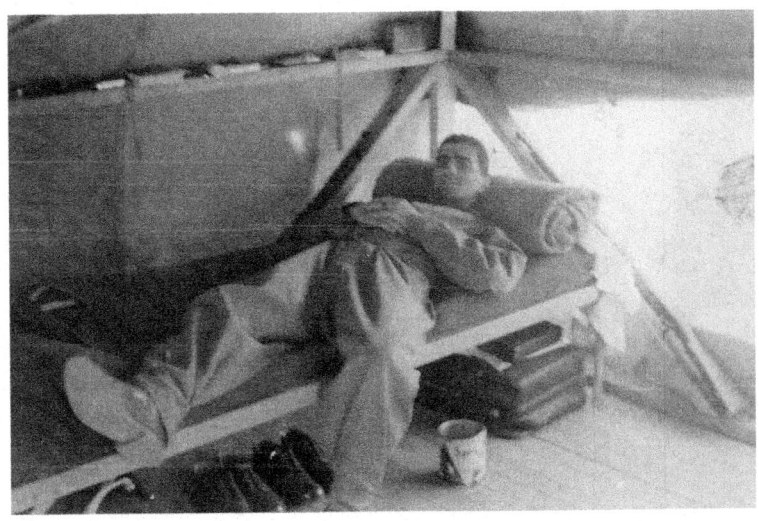

Above: This is a typical bunking area inside the tents. LaHurd's shoes, luggage and other personal belongings are neatly laid out. His monkey suit fits loosely over his body.

Left: LaHurd poses in his new uniform and holds his parade rifle. In the background is one of many double-decker barracks at SAAAB.

The cadets are packed up and ready to leave Santa Ana for Visalia, California.

LaHurd stands at attention in the center of the back row for mail call (Squadron 27).

Daniel LaHurd (*left*) and Tony Testa (*right*) stand in front of their barracks.

Chapter 3

AIRBORNE

June 24, 1942–August 30, 1942

The advent of air power, which can go straight to the vital centers and either neutralize or destroy them, has put a completely new complexion on the old system of making war. It is now realized that the hostile main army in the field is a false objective, and the real objectives are the vital centers.
—General Billy Mitchell

Just outside Visalia, a small airstrip known as Sequoia Field had been transformed from an agricultural flight school into an army air base established to teach cadets the foundational knowledge of aerial combat and provide flight experience to help pilots survive over hostile skies. Here, dodos—cadets, nicknamed after the flightless and extinct bird—strived to become pilots and, as a result of their new role, achieve a promotion to second lieutenant. Becoming a lieutenant brought the prestige and privileges of an officer: higher pay, off-base liberties and additional respect. Sequoia Field was a place where a military boy turned into a military man.

For most, becoming a flyboy was a difficult yet thrilling feat. Flying was rare. In the '40s, most young Americans never reached heights above their second-story bedroom. Combat piloting was still a new and rudimentary field. Only a few decades earlier had men such as Giulio Douhet and General Billy Mitchell advocated for an offensive flying combat sector of the military. Douhet, the Italian airpower theorist and author of *The Command of the Air*, had laid out his model of airpower resting on the belief that *the striking force and magnitude of aerial offensives, considered from the standpoint of either material or moral significance, is far more effective than those of any other offensive yet known. A nation which has command of the air is in a position to protect its own territory from enemy aerial attack and even to put a halt to the enemy's auxiliary actions in support of his land and sea operations, leaving him powerless to do much of anything. Such offensive actions can not only cut off an opponent's army and navy from their bases of operations, but can also bomb the interior of the enemy's country so devastatingly that the physical and moral resistance of the people would also collapse.*

Douhet had understood that this third dimension allowed the military to quickly and freely move in all directions with limited obstacles. If a military could go on the offensive, destroy consumer goods and diffuse civilian morale into submission, it would win wars. Douhet had understood that attacking the nucleus of an enemy's military—factories, civilian infrastructures, oil refineries, trains, etc.—was more devastating than dropping bombs on soldiers crouching in trenches on the front lines.[*]

U.S. General Billy Mitchell had shared a common military tactical belief: the third dimension of the air would be the futuristic means of military domination. He had verbally attacked both the United States War and Navy Departments for their lack of air superiority and outdated equipment. He postulated that the First World War was not the "war to end all wars" and urged the United States to update its air forces.[†]

Throughout the late 1920s and 1930s, the importance of air superiority had grown. However, at the dawn of the Second World War, America's third dimension had been substandard to its enemies. The intensification and expansion of U.S. aerial warfare had become crucial, and it all needed to start with well-trained soldiers.

Primary flight school was a laborious and difficult process, challenging each flyboy mentally and physically. A common joke describing the classroom hours was, "If you drop a pencil, by the time you reach to retrieve it, you might miss a whole semester." One of Daniel's classmates wrote, "Little did we dream that to gain a commission in the Army Air Force we were expected not only to out fly anything with wings but also to become human reservoirs of any and all knowledge connected, however remotely, with aeronautics."

---

[*] This theory was devised just after the First World War, when trench warfare was most salient in military strategy.

[†] Billy Mitchell prophesized the Second World War and the attacks on Pearl Harbor.

Those who passed primary training moved on to basic flight school. At basic, the men would school themselves in every aspect regarding flight and practice maneuvers within their specified aircraft. Those who failed were placed in E Company, transferred out and taught new skills to become useful in other facets of the war.

On the morning of June 27, 1942, Daniel awoke inside his new barracks and prepared himself for the grueling day. The living quarters at Sequoia Field surpassed the barracks, and certainly the tents, at SAAAB with regard to accommodations and functionality. The only real problem was swarms of massive flies that buzzed around the stucco building's interior. LaHurd and his ten roommates had hung a collage of fly paper from the ceiling in hopes of ridding their sleeping quarters of the buzzing intruders. The air conditioners in the rooms did little to cool the men from the outside temperatures of sometimes 120-degree heat. Inside, there were two showers, four wash bowls, personal clothes lockers, individual private desks and double-decker beds. With the additional amenities, the attention paid to order and cleanliness increased exponentially in comparison to Santa Ana. Every element was scrutinized, and only perfection was accepted.

LaHurd made sure to wake up on time at primary. The punishment for sleeping in late was not latrine duty like at SAAAB but instead two hours of running under the blazing sun. He quickly dressed, organized his footlocker and made his bed to the exact specifications of his instructor. The bed's sheet corners were precisely folded and tightly tucked. Making his bed was the toughest thing that Daniel found thus far in the military. "It took us fellows about an hour to make our beds today and tomorrow I'll have to get up about 45 minutes earlier to make my bed and fall out in time. Seems like we burn all of our energy making beds, kinda makes me hungry," he wrote to his parents. LaHurd had claimed a lower bunk, which was at least easier.

After an hour of calisthenics, Daniel's craving for food was satisfied. Breakfast could not have come fast enough for the cadet's starving stomach. A loaded plate of eggs, sausage, oatmeal, toast and bacon sat on a tray, with orange juice, milk and coffee.

For the first month of training, Daniel and the other cadets' eating habits were regulated by the upperclassmen. Sequoia Field had very few officers on base. Here, the cadets were managed by a unique system where the more experienced trainees ran the show. During the summer months at Sequoia Field, there were approximately twenty West Point cadets at primary flight training. The new cadets looked up to them and recognized that "they knew their stuff." The cadets were ranked as captain, lieutenant sergeant and so forth. The higher-ranked cadets had more experience and more knowledge. Their word was law, and it was compulsory to salute them and address them as sir.

Daniel sat at the chow table with three upperclassmen. Instead of grabbing his breakfast and shoving it down like a starving animal, he sat at attention on the front three to four inches of his chair, looked straight ahead and ate his food by bringing his utensil to his mouth in ninety-degree motions. His left hand rested in his lap, only to be used when cutting meat or buttering bread. This treatment lasted for a month. In addition to these particular eating instructions, Daniel had to jog double time to every destination on base. Dodos were forbidden to walk and had to salute every senior enlisted man on base as they jogged by.

After finishing his breakfast, LaHurd fell out to the tarmac. The day before, he and the other dodos had met their instructors for the first time. The veteran instructors had walked their groups around the aircraft, showing them the different parts of the plane. They also explained the parachute.

Each instructor had been assigned five dodos. These dodos listened to their new instructor's every word, for those words could soon mean life or death. LaHurd's instructor had spent the better part of the day explaining and discussing banks, patterns and wind directions. Daniel explained in a letter home that night, "After the instructor got done talking I didn't know if I was coming or going but all I can do is my best." Before dismissal, the dodos were given books for ground school that contained maps, charts, engine diagrams, diagnostics and calculation tables.

LaHurd had been assigned to fly first among his group. By 10:30 a.m., the sun was baking the desert floor. Dust blew across the flat, open expanse of the base. The air was dry. The base was only a short drive from Death Valley, where temperatures are known to reach triple digits on a regular basis, and there had not been a drop of rain for months. Each breath seemed to inhale more dust and heat than oxygen.

After two hours of instructions ranging from weather patterns to flight maneuvers, the group was prepared for their individual training flights. The men dressed in monkey suits. Their goggles, flight jackets, coveralls and flight caps made them look as though they were seasoned veterans.

Daniel jogged toward the aircraft with shaking legs. He wasn't sure if his knocking knees meant that he was nervous as hell or excited as hell or a little of both. The dodos he left behind, safely planted on earth, were cheering him on as he climbed into a Ryan PT-22 Trainer. The monoplane was the cadets' learning instrument, helping them cultivate basic stick and rudder flying. Capable of reaching altitudes over fifteen thousand feet, the Trainer was quite a ride for any undeveloped flyboy. Its immaculate, silver aluminum exterior reflected the early afternoon sun like a mirror. Its yellow wings and tail reminded everyone that it was a primary training vehicle.

Daniel strapped himself safely into the cockpit. His instructor found his own seat directly in front of the cadet. Captain Taggart's body was put together like an oak tree stump. The man barely possessed a neck. It was as if his head joined his shoulders—nothing in between. Veins in his forehead bulged as he barked orders at the dodo seated behind him. He acted more like a marine drill sergeant than an AAF flight instructor.

"Snap that strap on the double! Make it tighter! Tighter! Put your damn goggles over your god damn eyes you damn dodo," Taggart yelled. Daniel knew this scheduled forty-five-minute flight was going to seem much longer considering the tirades he was expecting from the rigorous instructor sitting in front.

Nothing seemed to be right, and the "damn" plane hadn't even moved an inch. The microphone system amplified the instructor's voice, making it even more irritating.

After a few routine flight checks, the aircraft began to taxi to the opposite end of one of the six parallel runways making up Sequoia Field. Taggart was in complete control of the aircraft and would remain in control throughout takeoff. At full throttle, the instructor finished his turn, aiming the nose of the plane down the runway. The PT-22 quickly accelerated toward the afternoon sun. Not knowing where the runway ended due to the blinding rays of sunlight, LaHurd was "damn" glad that Taggart was in full control of the plane. Over the popping noise of the engine, Daniel tried to listen to Taggart spit lessons on takeoff procedures. Trying to concentrate on what Taggart was yelling, along with worrying about the remaining distance of the runway and whether or not this was the end of his life, Daniel had a difficult time comprehending any useful knowledge for his next flight, one where he would be in full control of the aircraft from takeoff to landing.

The aircraft gained the required speed of eighty miles per hour for liftoff, and within seconds, the Trainer left the runway, heading toward the heavens. LaHurd thought he had left his stomach on the tarmac as the plane swiftly climbed to one thousand feet. The young cadet from Akron, Ohio, was now flying over California with an unimaginable view. The visibility was endless, obscured only by the blue atmosphere and the brown horizon meeting off in the distance. A cloudless sky made for a perfect view. To the east, mountains spiked from the ground. It was an unforgettable sight. For a brief moment, the noise of the engine, the screams from no-neck, the fear of being in an aluminum can high above the earth—all was forgotten. The joy of flying was the only thought in the dodo's mind. But that interval of calm was brief, very brief.

Captain Taggart ordered Daniel to take over the controls. Reaching down with sweaty palms, Daniel held the aircraft level. Bouncing around in a PT-22 for forty-five minutes was comparable to an arduous eight-hour day at a factory. Flying seemed to be such a difficult skill to acquire. However, after a little finesse, Daniel's fear of the unknown turned into excitement. He wrote home, "When we first leveled the ship I looked down and thought to myself, 'What if Taggart would tell me to jump' why I would have told him to go to hell and stuck with that little Ryan come hell or high water."

LaHurd pulled back on the stick, and the plane ascended to four thousand feet. Feeling comfortable, Daniel started specific maneuvers ordered by the instructor. The plane was at the mercy of Daniel's every move. Left turns, right turns, gliding turns, climbs and dives were on the agenda. Daniel did a fine job.

After the allotted time, he made his final approach to the runway. The plane slowly descended. LaHurd's gliding turns gradually decreased the plane's altitude from 4,000 feet to 3,000 feet to 2,000 feet to 1,500 feet. Finally, the instructor took control of the aircraft at 1,000 feet, maneuvering the plane on line with the landing strip. Taggart suddenly yanked the stick hard, turning the aircraft into a double twist, and then dropped the aircraft to 500 feet in a matter of a few seconds. Daniel thought his stomach was going to pop out of his skin. Dizziness set in. His entire body was suffused with a cold sweat. Another quick drop in altitude, followed by a tight spin, led to another bubble in LaHurd's stomach. That delicious breakfast consumed earlier moved around unpredictably inside him. With no hope of holding out until touchdown, he finally succumbed to the nausea of airsickness. Chunks of bacon, sausage and scrambled eggs mixed with milk and coffee sprayed forward until the outside draft caught the slime and accelerated it backward. He finally understood the true benefit of his goggles. He became suspicious of the intent of Taggart's double barrel roll, considering he was safely seated ahead of the dodo's position.

LaHurd was responsible for cleaning the aircraft before the next dodo jumped in and most likely had the same problem. Airsickness was a common occurrence for cadets on their first few missions. LaHurd's first bout of it was acceptable, but he only had five hours of flight time to correct the problem or he would be washed out.

Two days after Daniel's first flight, he wrote home informing his family about his piloting skills:

Mon. June 29, 1942
Visalia, California

Dear Folks

I went up at 8:27 this morning and stayed up till 9:12 A.M. total of 45 minutes and a grand total of 1 hour and 20 minutes in the air so far. Today we did power stalls and gliding stalls. I know you don't know what I mean but neither do I, I'm just telling you what the instructor told me. In power stall the ship is in a climb in fact a steep climb and when the ship loses power the nose falls and my job was to straighten it out by keeping the wings level and the nose on the horizon, some job. When that ship falls it's just like falling through space. We also did 45 turns left + right and what not. To tell you the truth I'll never be a pilot the way they want you to fly. They go so darn fast in teaching you, for example after a grand total of 1 hr. + 20 minutes in the air I am now ready to take the ship off tomorrow of course the instructor is in the front seat to help and boy! he's going to help me plenty. The last class that graduated from here 50% washed out and from the coming class to graduate I know of another little boy that's going to washout, that's right me. My stomach stayed in today but it darn near came flowing in my face again but I held it back just long enough. So far I'm not crazy about flying but maybe I'll like it better after I know a little more about it.

I'm glad to hear you've cut down on your gambling but the next time there's a Dan in a race [horse race] *lay off as my luck sure has been bad lately. By the way that $50 I sent home wasn't from winning at dice that was strictly pay money from dear old U.S.A. It sure is lucky I sent it home or I would have lost it at dice. Everything is under control and feeling swell but that heat is sure terrific out here. I weighed myself yesterday and I weighed 163 in the nude, not bad.*

144 lbs at Camp Perry
152 lbs the last time at Santa Ana
163 lbs. at Sequoia Field (Visalia, Cal)

Love + Kisses to All
Dan

He was flying almost daily. Each cadet was required to complete sixty hours of flight time to advance from primary training to basic training. The average duration per flight was forty-five minutes, requiring each cadet to partake in about eighty flights. The more often they flew, the faster they could get on to the next level and ultimately overseas to the real noise. After his fifth flight, giving him a combined total of three hours and thirty-six minutes, Daniel was no more confident as a pilot than he had been the day he rode the train into Visalia. He explained this lack of confidence in his next few letters home:

Thurs. July 2, 1942
Visalia, California

Dear Folks

This is hot pilot LaHurd giving you the details of today's flight. We went up at 9:15 A.M. to 10:00 A.M. and in the 45 minutes I was up you'd think I could learn a little but after my instructor gets done telling me the things I did wrong, I'm positive I knew more about flying before I was up in a plane then I do now. I never new one could make so many mistakes in only 3 hrs. + 36 minutes of total flying time but I guess I did.

Today we did our regular banks, turns, power stalls, gliding turns, climbing turns and today he made me go into a spin and pull out of it. We also had to take off twice and land twice but the instructor just sits in the front cockpit and tells you what to do and boy! his voice really hits a high tone when you do something wrong and after a few times more with me I'm afraid he is going to lose it. His voice I mean. My one landing was pretty good up to the point when the wheels hit the ground but after that the plane was on the ground doing about 80 miles per hr. it just wanted to go from one side of the field to the other but with the instructors help and my brains we got it under control. The planes are sure honeys and they practically fly themselves if you let lose of the controls but you'll never learn to control them if you let them fly themselves that's what the instructor says, anyhow. The only great danger is crashing into another plane and that is very unlikely as they always make you look around before turning or making any other maneuvers and if you don't look, ouch! my eardrums.

I hope you have a swell time at Al's and here's hoping you clean up at poker. I know darn well your not going all the way to Detroit and to Als and not playing poker.

51

I'm looking forward to getting the "Goodies" and thanks loads. If you didn't send the cigarettes yet, please don't as I want to try to cut down on my smoking and if I have plenty around I'll smoke plenty.

Feeling swell and hope all of you are feeling as well as I am but not as hot. Mike catch me a nice big pike and send me a picture of it.

Love
Dan

———

Fri. July 3, 1942
Visalia, California

Dear Folks

Well your letters have been coming everyday now so thanks for the good work. I received Cal's +Fred's letters today and glad to know they like their schoolwork. So college is easier than High school well just wait Fred, it'll start to get tough but keep at it and lets see you boys go all the way through not like your big brothers. Glad to hear you boys like your R.O.T.C. course, that gives you a general idea what I have to go through everyday. Drill and more drill. When I get home you boys can give me a few lessons in marching as half the time I don't know left from right but neither do most of the other fellows.

Today we only got 32 minutes in the air, today as our instructor has us fellows about 1 hour ahead of the other groups so now we have to slow down and let them catch up. The time we are suppose to have after Mondays flying is 3 hrs + 30 minutes and to date we have about 3 hrs + 32 minutes so you see we are ahead just a little bit and a little is a great deal in flying time.

I seem to be getting worse instead of better. I guess I wasn't made to be a flyer. "Santa Ana here I come." I think I'll go back to Santa Ana and be a bombardier this flying is no fun. I thought piloting a plane would be fun but not for me for the simple reason there is too much work involved and you know how I like work.

So Ma is going to school, Swell! and I hope she keeps it up and will wait for her first letter and frame it. Well I have to close now as formation for school is in 4 minutes.

Love
Dan

P.S. We get a 48 hr. pass because of 4th of July.

In July, Daniel was not only absent from home for Independence Day but was also away during his mother's, father's and sister's birthdays. He wrote to his father, "Give Ma a big birthday kiss for me and have her kiss you for me for your birthday present. You good people are having a lot of birthdays, three in a week, good going. Tell Lou I wish her all the luck in the world on the 28th birthday. Pretty soon she'll be as young as Ma. Do people still think they are sisters?"

By LaHurd's seventh flight, his frustrations were mounting. He just couldn't get Taggart off his back. He wrote to his father:

> Well after my flight today I was ready to quit but I'll give it a couple more days' trial. Whoever told me I could fly? They're going to have to build a special plane for me, one with three cockpits so I will have another place for one more instructor because it takes about two good men to take down and correct all the mistakes I make. This flying is no fun and I'm under a serious strain all the time I'm in the air. I guess my biggest trouble is I'm trying too hard and am not relaxed but what's the difference this war will probably end soon. Except for my flying everything else is O.K. so no need to worry about a thing as everything will come out for the best.

Of course, the war would last another three years and LaHurd would find himself right in the heart of it. But first he had to figure out how to land the PT-22. Without that important skill, he wouldn't be able to go up solo, and if he couldn't go up solo, his days as a pilot were numbered. He wrote home:

> We flew this morning and I still can't land that plane consistently. I'll land it good once and the next time I'll bounce all over the field. Seeing that I couldn't land that little Ryan I told the instructor he best give me a check ride and wash me out so Monday I'll get it, I mean the check ride. My air work is good but if I can't land the plane it's no use of fooling around. When I get home I'll take you for a plane ride but you'll have to jump to get back to good old terra firma. I learned that in high school. Latin I hope.

LaHurd's days at Sequoia Field were dwindling. About 40 percent of his class had already been washed out and sent back to Santa Ana; 10 percent more would wash out before the group finished at primary. Included in that 10 percent was Daniel. The army board finally declassified him, and he would soon return to Santa Ana.

Anxious to fight for his country and gain some real combat experience, Daniel feared that he might miss the war altogether if he continued to train in the States. He also felt somewhat defeated by the airplane and a little upset at the fact that he wouldn't become a revered pilot. The next best thing to wearing a military uniform was having wings pinned to it; the ladies went crazy over American flyboys. LaHurd was going to have to find his niche in the air force and soon.

Mon. July 20, 1942
Visalia, California

Dear Folks

I had my semi official last ride today and tomorrow I will get my last official ride and then my career as a pilot will come to a close.

Sunday morning my buddy and I were coming back from Tulare and we saw B25 and Hudson bombers at the bomber base so we got off the bus and got permission from one of the officers to look at them which we did and are they honeys. They have more darn guns on them. They have a 30 Cal. gun on each side of middle + a 50 Cal. gun in the rear + a 50 Cal in the nose, it's well protected. We then got permission to take a ride in a B25 and we went to Fresno + back about 100 miles round trip and it was really fun. I laid in rear end and could see everything as we passed over. We were up for about 35 minutes and could have went up again but we had to get to our "Country Club." This morning one of the B25 at that base crashed. It caught on fire at the take off and before it could go very far it was a dead duck, all those damn good men gone. Sometimes we don't realize war over there kills good men over here.

I received the pictures of the kids and also yours in the paper and they are swell. Tell Beulah that I showed the pictures she took to the captain and he is going to see if he can get her in the observation corp and take pictures for the army. I still liked them and will be waiting for more.

Feeling swell.

Love + Kisses
Dan

P.S. Army made us take pictures in our flight suits as they want three for I don't know what so I'm having a few made to send home. Enclosed is a couple of proofs I snuck out. I look like a fat little pig

The trip up in the B-25 may have been the defining moment for him. He loved the plane's sheer size and was awestruck by the number of guns

A Ryan PT-22 trainer sits on the tarmac at Sequoia Field.

fortifying it. His interest quickly moved from being a fighter pilot to finding his role on a bomber. He knew that he didn't want to be a gunner, and he had already learned that piloting was out of the question. After talking to some of the commanders, he learned more details about the bombardier and navigator positions and quickly became intrigued.

LaHurd's final declassification orders came, and he was ordered back to SAAAB. He walked to the main highway outside Visalia, and before he could even put up his thumb to hail a ride, he was picked up by a doctor and his son heading to Los Angeles. The three men traveled the two hundred miles together.

Daniel wrote home:

> *The Doc was a pretty nice guy, he bought me a chicken dinner and gave me his card and told me to call him sometime and he would take me around. I could have gone deep sea fishing with him today but I have to report back at Santa Ana at 10:00 p.m. He told me I was a real hero and not to worry about pilot. He told me to find a position I like because who knows how long this damn war will last.*

After a respectful handshake with the doctor, Daniel made his way to SAAAB to continue his search for his role in the AAF.

Chapter 4

SQUARE ONE

August 31, 1942–December 31, 1942

Air power is like poker. A second-best hand is like none at all—it will cost you
dough and win you nothing.
—*General George Kenney*

LaHurd sat in his bunk slightly inclined from two pillows that supported his back. His feet were covered by a blanket, shielding them against the unusually cool air. It had been nearly four months since he hitched a ride with the doctor and his son down the coastline of California to Santa Ana Army Air Base. Daniel's room inside a double-decker barracks was shared with three other cadets. The wooden interior was spacious and clean except for the dusty floors. A stale smell hung in the air, a citrusy mildew. Outside, a sea of plain brown dust stretched to the horizon. Fortunately, this particular barracks, a new building, had green grass surrounding the outside. It was nice to look out the window and see greenery as a substitute for ordinary dirt and dust. Plus, the grass kept the mud down on rainy days. But the real perk of the barracks was its running hot water, something the older buildings lacked.

He grabbed a pen and a few pieces of paper, a commodity in short supply, from his footlocker that sat in front of his bunk. He absentmindedly scribbled drawings of airplanes, women's legs and a royal flush across a sheet of paper. Across the room, five of his buddies knelt around a bunk, laughing and joking. Playing cards and money were spread out over a mattress. The game was poker, an everyday ritual for the future airmen.

Daniel wrote to his family: "The boys have been playing cards like mad around here. They even miss mess and when they would rather play cards than eat, well...that's bad." Cards and gambling washed away melancholy spirits. The real world filled with grueling training, homesickness and the inevitability of war vanished from each cadet's mind when the playing cards were dealt. The only thing they had to worry about at that moment was the bluff, not where they would be stationed, how long it would be until they saw their family again or if they would die. The improvised poker tables, craps tables and blackjack tables personified freedom like nothing else in the military. Here, soldiers were no longer soldiers—they were just boys, boys without title, without rank, and their precarious futures were forgotten for at least a moment. The only rules: cheating and war talk were forbidden. As a result, conversation tended to skew toward ladies, hometown memories and sports.

Hundreds of dollars were won and lost by soldiers at these poker games over the course of their service. Among these spendthrifts, a paramount gambler was LaHurd. His paychecks could be doubled, tripled or lost entirely in any given game. The cadets frequently looked over and pleaded for LaHurd's participation. They knew he was always good for a handful of jokes. His suave stories about the ladies were almost as entertaining as the card game itself.

But today he opted out of the day's game. It was Thanksgiving, and contrary to his jovial personality and gambling addiction, the only thing he could think about was his family. He just wanted to be with them on this special holiday. Many things had changed over the past eight months. His depressing thoughts deepened as he thought about how he would also be absent for Christmas and New Year's.

As the men continued with their game, Daniel pulled out a new sheet of paper and began to write home. Each of his promised letters proved to be an exhausting task. Only a diminutive amount of information could be put into each letter for fear of classified information halting the delivery of it from military control into civilian hands. Government censorship was extremely stubborn. For this reason, Daniel chose to limit details instead of risking his letters' eradication. An additional challenge in writing was to keep depressing circumstances and pessimistic thoughts to a minimum in order to keep up morale.

Thurs. Nov. 26, 1942
Santa Ana, California

Dear Folks

Here it is "Thanksgiving Day" and I'm some 2500 miles from home. This is probably the first time we all haven't had Thanksgiving dinner together but I'll be thinking of you as I bite into the white meat of the turkey.

I put in a nice day of K.P. duty Tues. I had two tables to wait on and did those 48 cadets keep me busy serving them. Then I had to clean the table, reset it, sweep and mop around it for six meals.

Weds. all we did was drill and athletics and today we will probably have a parade and how we all hate that. I might not catch K.P. Sat. + if I don't I'm going to try to see the Notre Dame game.

I'm feeling swell and here's wishing you all a good "Thanksgiving." I hope we're all together next year.

Love + Kisses
Dan

LaHurd folded up his Thanksgiving letter, placed it into the addressed and stamped envelope and sealed the back. He pressed the envelope to his puckered lips, thought of his family and recalled the past few months at SAAAB.

Passing through the gates of the camp in early September for the second time, Daniel was amazed by its expansion. In the eastern section, multiple barracks were being constructed to accommodate the influx of cadets due to the expanding war effort and the growing necessity for aerial warriors. The United States Army Air Corps had been made up of 1,700 aircraft in 1939. By 1944, the United States Army Air Force built nearly one hundred times that number per year and grew to 80,000 planes and 2.4 million personnel. By D-day, the AAF made up 31 percent of the army's total strength and proliferated into the largest air force in the world. More planes pumped out of American factories than Britain, the Soviet Union, Germany and Japan combined. And all these planes needed pilots, copilots, radiomen, gunners, bombardiers, engineers, navigators, maintenance crews, radar men, flight instructors, classroom teachers and more. Additionally, all of these men required places to train, wash, eat and sleep. Santa Ana Army Air Base provided these facilities and accommodations. By the end of 1942, over

23,400 cadets had passed through the training facility at SAAAB. Only one year later, that number increased to a staggering 57,895 cadets. The AAF was growing fast, extremely fast.

LaHurd found his tent among the plethora of other tents and barracks. He was quickly appointed as tent captain, his tent's condition and organization resting solely on his shoulders.

The days were a bit boring. The fact that he had to start from scratch all over again made him feel a bit like a failure. No cadet wanted to go through those classroom hours again. No cadet wanted to pick up details like Fire Guard or Kitchen Patrol again. And surely, no cadet wanted to move from a nice air-conditioned stucco barracks to a tent that sat atop the dusty grounds of Santa Ana. Just like his first time here, he moved around like a pinball from tent to barrack and from barrack to tent. But he did experience a few new and agonizingly unique things his second time around. He was confronted with the pressure chamber. The cadets that couldn't handle the deprivation of adequate oxygen were washed out. Another unbearable experience was the chemical gas lectures. The instructors exploded several different tubes filled with chemical gas, and the cadets were ordered to walk through the clouds and inhale. The fumes had been irritatingly painful; nearly every cadet vomited, their eyes burned and watered, temporarily blinding them, snot and mucus ran from their mouths and noses and their throats burned as if they had drank bleach.

The shooting range was a great stress reliever. LaHurd was given the opportunity to shoot the Thompson submachine gun, and he wrote home telling his family about the experience: "Now I know why those Chicago gangsters felt so tough. We shot 12 rounds at semiautomatic and the other 22 rounds at full auto with bursts of three, any more than that and your gun would end up pointing at the sky."

Fri. Aug. 21, 1942
Santa Ana, California

Dear Folks
Well today I went into the pressure chamber after missing the last time I was here. They took us up to 5000 ft and back down in a hurry + the ones who can't stand it are let out of the pressure tank. We then are taken up to 18,000 ft. + at that height we put on our oxygen masks and are taken up to 28,000 ft. I was O.K. and it didn't bother me a bit although some fellows got dizzy and some had trouble making their eardrums pop.

We are having a practice evacuation tonight and the only ones to stay behind are fire guards + others who are necessary, such as guards. Lucky me, I'm on fire guard duty so I won't have to march ten miles like the other poor suckers and 100 fellows in our Co. have K.P. duty tomorrow and have to get up at 4:00 A.M., clear their tents and then go on K.P. duty for 16 hours after hiking 10 miles. Some fun. This fireguard is a snap. All you do is lay around and take it easy + you get out of all formations. I think I'll try to get it for a permanent position.

I'll probably be classified this coming Wed. as bombardier. You know that fellow who rides in the nose of the plane and drops those little eggs that go "BOOM."

I guess you found out by this time that working on the lawn isn't so easy. So now you can see why Fred, Cal + I always tried to duck it.

I have enough cash to last me a couple of weeks yet but if I need any I'll let you know.

Last Sat. I bought a pair of pants for $16 and are they nice. Ma probably will be sick when you tell her I paid that much but the Majors are no better than me + if they can wear them I guess I can to.

Tell Beulah I received her letter + thank her for me. So Ma is still going to school, well good for her. Has Ma flicked school yet? Tell her to try it because it's a lot of fun at least I used to think so.

Well I better close now and take a walk around the tents, at least once anyhow. That's why they left me here.

Love + Kisses to All

Dan

By September, he was reclassified as a bombardier. He started school again—the same subjects he had taken in the spring, but this time with the addition of meteorology. He desperately struggled with the subject and feared that if he failed he would wash out into the infantry.

Weds. Nov. 4, 1942

Santa Ana, California

Dear Folks

I only have a week and a half to go to school yet and am a little worried about flunking meteorology and if I do I'll become a buck ass private. They use to give you an extra three weeks of schooling if you flunk a subject but now they did away with that. I guess it's the old law of supply and demand. They have the supply + I want the demand. I'll know better after the final exam. Gosh! I never new what meteorology was till five weeks ago and I still don't.

The other night I sold a candy bar for a nickel and got into a poker game and won $15 without taking any money from my wallet so that just goes to show you, you can start in a poker game with a nickel but you best have some money on you or they just soon murder you as a Jap around here. Last night I won another forty dollars which isn't too bad for the week and now I can play the rest of the month on their money, for a change. I'm enclosing another $20 money order and have two made out to me for a total of $40. Just for safety sake so I won't lose it before the months over. I also have $40 in my pocket in cash and $10 loaned out. I've done pretty well so far this month. Lets hope my luck stays good.

I go back to drilling and athletics tomorrow as my darn big toe feels normal again. Darn it, I never have any luck. I was hoping it would be sore for at least two weeks but no, it had to get better.

Glad to hear Fred the "Lover" had a good time with <u>our</u> blonde.

Love + Kisses

Dan

The overall highlight of autumn for Daniel and his squadron was winning parade for their stellar performance on the parade ground. Winning the white banner meant the group would receive perks all week until another group took the honor the following week. LaHurd and the other cadets were spoiled for seven days. They were served steak dinners with salad, green beans, potatoes, cake and ice cream. Daniel wrote home, "Good thing I wasn't flying in that damn Ryan Trainer with that meal in my stomach or the steak would have been flying through the air."

The white banner holders were also given front-row seats to Eddie Cantor's broadcast on the base. For LaHurd, the front row gave him a better view of Dinah Shore, Eddie Cantor's guest for the night, and Daniel didn't take his eyes off of her the entire show. He wrote to his brother Calvin, "Miss Shore can park her shoes under my bed anytime."

Daniel also enjoyed the visit by General Henry Harley "Hap" Arnold. He and his roommates had spent the morning cleaning up their room for Hap's visit, just in case the general decided to walk in. General Arnold was known to be a driven and ruthlessly impatient man. Arnold's staff described him as a "slave driver" who had once killed a man with his words: a lower-level staff officer had had a heart attack and died right in front of Hap's desk after a particularly harsh tirade. Although he was rigidly strict and authoritative, he was also an ingenious strategist and august leader. When this paragon of what an airman should be walked past LaHurd's barracks, LaHurd gave the general a crisp salute.

Daniel kissed the envelope that held his Thanksgiving letter home and walked it over to the post office. He then made his way to the mess hall for Thanksgiving dinner. The cadets were fortunate to have a swell supper: nuts, bananas, grapes, apples, pumpkin pie, fruit cake, candied sweet potatoes, salad, pickles, green onions, celery, lettuce, radishes, turkey and dressing, milk, coffee, ice cream and fruit juice. The best part of the meal: no limitation on the amount of food to be consumed.

Back in his barracks, appetite satisfied, he grabbed the local *Beacon Journal*, sent from home, and thumbed through the pages. The news was usually a few days late, consequences of delayed mail from Akron to Santa Ana. He skipped over the headlines on death tolls, battles, politics and conquered lands. Most entertaining was the news about football, predominantly college football. His home state was ranked second in the country behind Georgia. Daniel followed the Ohio State Buckeyes' progress intimately as the team went on to finish the season with a nine-and-one record and earn its first title as national champions, led by Coach Paul Brown.

Sun. Nov. 29, 1942
Santa Ana, California

Dear Folks

We had an early inspection Sat. and got to leave the post early, in fact early enough to buy four of the last ten tickets for the Notre Dame game. The tickets cost $3.30 apiece and was glad to pay it as that was my only chance to see a football game this year and besides I always wanted to see N.D. play. It was a pretty fair game and a few good plays pulled but than I'm not able to judge how good of a game it was as I can't compare it with any other game I saw. So I'll have to say it was the best game I saw this year.

I'm broke again. The first time in a month or so but than we get paid tomorrow for the rest of the month. We got a partial payment about two weeks ago of $29 so we'll have about $42 coming.

Tell Ma I still have some cookies but I still would rather have Buttelaywee (I hope you can make out what I mean). Just a few pieces will satisfy me.

There isn't anything I can use in the way of clothing so don't spend any money buying me things. I have more clothes now than I can keep clean.

Friday I went through all the letters you wrote me and glanced over them again and had to throw them away as I had to many to carry from barrack to barrack and from place to place when I move and they sure keep moving you.

Pa no one from this post is given a furlough unless there is a death or serious illness in the family and I'd rather never go home under those conditions. I'll probably get a furlough after I graduate from advance training school and that will be in four months at the most. This war can't last much longer as I've been in 8 months now and I never did hold a job over a year so I give the war four more months and if it doesn't end than I'll set a new record of holding a job for over a year.

Pa please answer these questions for me in your next letter.

Date of your Birthday
Date of Ma's Birthday
Lou's age 28—Born July 19, 1914
Mike's age 26—Born March 22, 1916
Cal's age 18—Born March 10, 1924
Fred's age 20—Born November 24, 1922
If you know off hand the addresses where we lived in Lorain + Detroit
Mr. Outland's address 211 Castle Blvd, Akron, Ohio
Mr. Calvert's address 2322 Grant St. Cuyahoga Falls, Ohio
(I used their names as references so please tell them I did and hope its O.K. I also used Dr. Allen.)

We had to fill out a form of some 84 questions and I wasn't sure of the above. I believe its for the FBI.

I'm feeling swell but a little tired after a wild weekend.

Love + Kisses
Dan
Say hello to All

The FBI would check on Daniel and his family to ensure that he was suited to use one of the most secret weapons of the Second World War, the Norden Bombsight. If things checked out with the government, LaHurd would be off to advanced training to become a bombardier.

By December 8, 1942, the United States had been entrenched in war for a year. LaHurd wrote to his family:

I can hardly believe those damn Japs bombed us a year ago. Well, they are getting what they deserve and they aren't going to last long against this machine of a military. Time sure is going fast. Can you believe a year ago most Americans didn't even know what Japan was. Now their brothers + husbands + fathers are all over the damn Pacific Ocean on little islands fighting little Japs.

Christmas came just as fast as 1942 went. LaHurd was still waiting to ship out for advanced. He received a Sheik electric razor as a Christmas gift from his family. He had sent home a leather jacket and a set of bombardier wings for his little nephew Neil and two dresses for his nieces Linda Lou and Mary Lou. He had also sent money home to his sister Louise and asked that she buy Pa Joe, Ma, his brothers and herself something nice.

Xmas—1942
Santa Ana, California

Dear Folks

I just received four letters from home and that's about the best present I could receive. I also received letter from Mike + Louise yesterday.

I know I haven't been writing too regular but I don't have much to write about for the simple reason we do the same thing everyday.

Hey! Cal, I sure hope you flunk your physical with flying colors. I like thinking that you are safe at home not marching in the military. So your girlfriend made your toes curl. Boy! she sure must be hot stuff. Have you + Fred learned to dance yet?

Fred your girlfriend is really cute but I thought you was running around with a blonde. Ah! what happened to the blonde love affair? You won't have it so bad in the army if your going with the rest of the fellows in the R.O.T.C. at least you'll know most of the fellows and my guess is you'll be put in a good branch of the service with the little training you already have.

I'm getting so use to this place now I kinda hate to leave it but the sooner I complete my training the sooner I might get a furlough and that is what I'm looking forward to.

I tried to call last night but there was a five hour delay and we wouldn't have made connection till about 3 A.M. so I'll try again this noon.

Last week when I found out we were to have a four day leave for Xmas, I started to plan how I could get home and eat Xmas dinner with all of you. I talked to another fellow from Penn. and we planned together and we almost made it. First we went down to the Municipal Airport in Long Beach and had them wir back east and reserve us seats coming back to the west coast, from there, we went to the Ferry Command but we were stopped at the gate

An endless line of tents sits in front of two-story barracks.

LaHurd lounges on a bunk, smoking a cigarette while doing leg lifts
during a transition from tent to barracks.

*by the guards but with a few lies we managed to get in. Everything looked
rosy as getting in was the hardest and the main thing in our plan. On getting
in we talked to a few pilots and they told us we needed chutes but hell they
were laying all around the place and need be, we would borrow a couple ,
of course, without their knowing it and would send them back upon arriving
at our destination. We could just see ourselves walking in the door back
home but the one thing we didn't plan was the weather and Wed. night it
began to rain and it continued all through Thurs. plus that it was foggy.
After planning how to get our chutes we went to the operations room and*

65

there, the world crumbled. "No flights today Mr., weathers too bad." Them words were heard and hurt us to the quick. You see the only passengers they're allowed to take are those connected with the "Ferry Command" but we could have snuck on a plane. Maybe it was all for the best because if we didn't get back here by Sunday 3 P.M. we would have been washed out but I was willing to take the chance. We did all this yesterday morning.

Hope you all have a really swell Xmas and I'll be thinking of you.

I tried to buy Ma a gift but I just couldn't find anything good enough but the first thing I see worth while I'll buy it for her.

Love + Kisses

Dan

Daniel continued to keep his fingers crossed that Calvin and Fred could somehow avoid the military. He hated to think that his little brothers could someday be fighting overseas. He grew sick at the thought of his mother having to bear each day with all her boys in action.

Just before the New Year, LaHurd was sent off to advanced training in Deming, New Mexico, and just before he left he wrote home, "All I know about the place is that it is close to NO WHERE. I guess we can spit across the Mexican border where we're going but anything will do to get out of here."

Chapter 5

EYE ON NORDEN

January 1, 1943–March 29, 1943

A modern, autonomous, and thoroughly trained Air Force in being at all times will not alone be sufficient, but without it there can be no national security.
—General Henry Harley "Hap" Arnold

D eming Air Field was erected from the New Mexican desert in 1942. The isolated airfield's only connection to the outside world was a single railroad track and a sandy road that stretched one hundred miles to the nearest city of El Paso, Texas. Its sole function was to train bombardiers for the Second World War. Deming was new; LaHurd's class was only the second to train there. By war's end, the instructors at Deming had trained approximately twelve thousand bombardiers.

The city of Deming, only a few miles from the airfield, was barely big enough to warrant a place on the map, its population only three thousand citizens. Occasionally, rumbles from bomber engines high above echoed through its streets. When cadets were not training, the city's streets were filled with a quiet stillness only interrupted by dry winds skipping grains of desert sand across the ground. It didn't provide much distraction for military men on weekend furloughs. LaHurd wrote home about the city, "I have never seen a sadder looking town in my life."

Daniel's barracks was a one-story structure, new but already sandblasted by the frequent desert sandstorms. His room housed himself and another cadet, Vincent "Ginks" Ginkus. Ginks was a "happy-golucky" guy. His good looks and confident demeanor made for a perfect match with LaHurd.

Ginks referred to LaHurd as "Danny Boy," and the two quickly bonded with a few other men in their barracks: Joseph Horvantz from Cleveland, Ohio; Emmett Killebrew from Dallas, Texas; and Irving Katz from New York City. Katz and the other four characters made up the Katz Klassy Klip Klub (KKKK). Word of the cabal spread around the airfield, and everyone wanted to be a member. When the KKKK hit the town on weekends, they had an absolute blast together. When they were stuck at Deming, they filled the voids of time with gambling, lots of gambling.

Other than Ginks, Daniel's room contained a table and chair, a gas heater and canvas cots. The barracks rooms were spare but comfortable. LaHurd was issued bedding, two blankets, one comforter, a pillow and pillow case, a mattress cover, a footlocker and sheets, all of which would be returned after the twelve weeks of training. The only drawback to the living quarters was the community latrines, a building that sat about fifty feet from the barracks. Routine sandstorms and chilly nights made for an uncomfortable walk to the bathroom. The wind over the open desert frequently whipped up sand, making the cadets' lives miserable. Sand blew into their rooms and accumulated everywhere. Oftentimes, a half inch of it built up on LaHurd's bed.

The airfield's acreage contained a theater, a chapel, a post office, a laundry room, six bowling alleys, a billiards table, a mess hall, a hospital, classrooms, hangars, repair shops, a giant checkered water tower, runways and a number of mysterious little concrete structures dispersed throughout the property. It wasn't long before LaHurd learned the purpose of the highly guarded concrete configurations. They were vaults containing one of the most highly classified secrets of World War II. The Norden Bombsights sat safely inside under twenty-four-hour security. They were protected from enemy bombs, unless directly hit, and secured from enemy spies and thieves. Each bombsight cost the military $10,000, and its offensive accuracy made it worth every penny. Each cadet, upon arriving at Deming Air Field, recited an oath swearing to protect the sight and its secrets with his life.

LaHurd wrote home, careful not to reveal any secretive information: "From what I hear the bombsight will do everything but cook, that is if you put the right calculations in it and that's what we have to learn in ground school."

The military and FBI were extremely vigilant about keeping the bombsight a secret from the enemy. All of the cadets' classroom notes and paperwork were confidential. Every paper was turned in and locked away in a safe by the instructor after each class. Any notes found on the cadets or in their rooms could lead to imprisonment. Daniel wrote home during his first week at the airfield, "I was going to tell you the new setup but I best not. I might get into trouble. I have to be careful what I write about, so you see it's pretty tough to write a letter and make it interesting."

Strategic bombing had increasingly become a necessity in the war. In order for the Allies to claim victory, they needed to bomb targets behind the front lines and strike the foundation of the Axis military: factories, oil refineries, bridges, marshaling yards and communication facilities. At Deming, the cadets learned how to accomplish that feat. Men were taught the basics of aerial bombing, target vulnerabilities, the functionalities of the classified and enigmatic bombsight, automatic piloting, loading and fusing of bombs, the destructive power of the armament, bombing probabilities, bombing errors, target identification and aircraft identification and navigational techniques.

Norden's bombsight provided the future bombardiers sighting accuracy, but the piece of equipment that would allow them to gain bombing experience was the Beech AT-11 aircraft. This double-engine trainer provided cadets with an aircraft that could reach a top speed of 215 miles per hour and climb to altitudes of twenty-two thousand feet. The belly of the plane could cradle ten one-hundred-pound bombs, and most importantly, its nose held the bombsight. One could say that Deming Air Field was built around the Beech AT-11 and the AT-11 was built around the Norden Bombsight.

Deming's bombardier training was categorized into three phases coupled with ground school and multiple hours on the ground trainer: Phase One—daylight bombing missions, Phase Two—night bombing missions and Phase Three—combat bombing missions. Classroom hours taught the fundamentals for aerial training. The instructors, all officers, wasted no time. The cadets were attending classes after their second day through the gates. Their schedule started with three two-hour classes, followed by two hours in a ground trainer, followed by hours of homework.

LaHurd understood the importance of class work. "Our very lives may depend on the knowledge we learn in these classes," he wrote. LaHurd wrote to his brother Calvin about maintenance school that taught the men the inner workings of the Norden Bombsight and how to make minor repairs to it. "Seems like they want us to learn how to drop bombs, fly the plane, and seems like they want us to learn how to build it and invent new parts."

Sunday Jan. 10, 1943
Deming, New Mexico

Dear Folks

I received all of the letters you addressed to Santa Ana and even though I got them late they were as good as if they just came off the fire. I know I haven't written for three days but I've been pretty busy studying and it did me some good as I got one of the highest grades in our class of 100 men. The test was fifty questions and some pretty tricky ones at that but they couldn't fool me. Next Sat. we will have a test in Theory of Bombsight and that is suppose to be a bitch. The way they work it here is they give you your test on Sat. and if you fail they give you a chance to make it up and if you fail the second time—well your through but I think it's fair. Hell if you can't pass it the second time you don't deserve another chance. We finished one week of school yesterday and so far I like it swell. Its got pilot training beat all over.

We had a stand by inspection yesterday and I got by without a "gig" I went bowling last night and really did lousy. The low men had to pay for the games and I only bowled four and paid for none so I had a cheap evening. I went to church again this morning. I'm getting to be a holy boy.

The weather here has been nice and brisk and we've had to wear our coats. Its not too cold but just right to give one a good appetite and I've been really putting the food away. The food is really good and they really pour it to us. We had pie four times last week, chicken once, turkey once, candy, nuts, pickles and etc. I hope it keeps up.

How about giving me a good resume of the Xmas presents received from Santa. Did Neil and the little girls receive their presents.

That's about it so, I'll close.

Feeling perfect.

Love + Kisses
XXXXXX Dan XXXXXX

P.S. Thanks a million for the swell birthday card and money.

Daniel had celebrated his twenty-fourth birthday on January 5. It was filled with classroom hours, athletics and ground training. He wrote home, "I made the twenty four year mark today and hope I can keep adding a year every year for some time. Hopefully this war doesn't ruin my plan."

Before allowing the cadets to enter the AT-11, the instructors required each to build up some simulated experience inside a ground trainer. The air force had developed a motor-driven simulator—essentially transformed military jeeps seating a driver, an instructor and a bombardier in training. The student sat in the back with a bombsight. In front of the jeep was another motorized device about a foot square that acted as the target. While one student was practicing, the other was driving. The students were required to spend twenty hours in the simulator before going up and attempting the real thing. At first, the cadets had a hell of a time with the ground trainer. There were even rumors that aerial bombing was easier than the simulated bombings from within the transformed jeep. After LaHurd had accumulated ten hours in the trainer, he finally felt that he was getting the knack and feel for the job.

The twelve-week training session pushed the men to their mental and physical thresholds. Each phase was considered completed after fifty bombs had been dropped. Success was measured by passing grades in class, meeting or surpassing time on the ground trainer and beating the benchmark or average curve for circular error on bombing runs.

The circular error had originally been set at 270 feet when LaHurd arrived at Deming but was lowered to 230 feet just after his first bombing run. Unfortunately, this made things even more complicated. If he didn't attain a direct hit on the target, he had to come within 230 feet of it on average to complete his training. To make matters even more difficult, the cadets had to multiply their score by a converging factor of 1.92. Therefore, in actuality, the cadet had to come within 120 feet of the target to make the average curve of 230 feet. LaHurd knew that one bad day or a wild bomb had the potential of destroying his overall average.

The magic number for him over the next twelve weeks was 230 feet. If he couldn't make the grade, he would be washed out. If he made the grade, he would move on as a bombardier and become an officer, a second lieutenant.

His first flight was a dry run designed to expose him to real bombing runs and get him into the air and comfortable with flying. Most cadets had never gone to pilot school, so the original dry run was their first airborne experience. During dry runs, the cadets never dropped bombs; they simply performed mock bombing raids. The crew consisted of a pilot, instructor and two students. Eventually, the instructors would stay grounded while the trainers went up for solo practice. While one student practiced dropping bombs, usually five bombs per mission, the other student took pictures of the attack through a small hole in the belly of the aircraft. The film was later studied to perfect the student's techniques.

LaHurd wrote home about his failed endeavor as a photographer:

Well the very first picture I took of the other cadets bombs—I held the trigger on the camera from the time the bomb left the plane till it hit and that was at 4000 ft. I used 180 frames where as about 4 frames would do the trick. You're supposed to snap the picture when the bomb hits and flashes. Of course I was called in to explain and I did. We use movie cameras and you just have to touch the trigger and here I let my finger rest on it and didn't know I was putting pressure on it. I think I'll have the film shown in Hollywood, BOMBS AWAY by D.E. LaHurd.

His superiors were furious that he had wasted so much film, and he sat through his instructor's tirades. LaHurd and the other members of **KKKK** had a good laugh about the error that evening.

The pilot flew the plane at four thousand feet above the ground. From this altitude, the targets below looked miniature, and LaHurd had his doubts of whether he'd be able to put a bomb close to them. His second time in the air was real; bombs were going to fall from the belly of the airplane. He hopped into the plane and prepared his instruments using the knowledge learned on the ground trainer and in the classroom. The pilot succeeded in getting the loaded double-engine bomber airborne. LaHurd knew what a chore it was to take off and land an airplane, and he never took the pilot's ability to do so for granted. He briefly thought about Taggart back at Visalia as the AT-11 leveled off at four thousand feet.

Turbulence rattled the warship as it approached the designated target. The riveted metal sheets that made up the body of the aircraft strained to hold together as the bomber forced its way through the air. The rocky, arid earth below moved by in a blur of browns and tans. Dispersed mesquite trees created shady black splotches throughout the desert, whose only inhabitants were scorpions, rattlesnakes, sparse rodents and the occasional roadrunner.

Today's mission: destroy an enemy target at a low-level altitude approach. LaHurd, only minutes out from the target, continued to run through his checks and balances. His dials, switches, controls, linkages, releases and racks needed to be attuned to ensure complete destruction of the target. He was anxious to see what the bombsight was really made of. Crammed in his vibrating glass and aluminum pod, LaHurd's hands trembled, his heart thumped and his breathing escalated.

The pilot transferred the controls of the aircraft over to the bombardier. Until "Bombs Away" crackled through the static-filled communication system, the bombardier was the commanding officer onboard. Never before had LaHurd been so nervous and downright anxious in his life. Screwing this up and becoming a private was merely a miscalculation away. The cadets were taught in class that the success of any bombing mission rested solely on the precision and accuracy of the bombs. All other activities— navigation, piloting, engineering and communications—were secondary to the destruction of the target.

LaHurd adjusted his Norden Bombsight, compensating for altitude, speed, bomb ballistics, trail, groundspeed and drift.* Charts and tables helped him understand these different elements. Dials and switches were correctly altered to balance the physics. Bombing was not a perfected art. Every number, each turn of the dial and a bit of luck determined whether the mission ended as a success or failure.

The average bombing accuracy over the course of the war was approximately three-quarters of a mile. Here at Deming, LaHurd needed that circular error to be less than 230 feet. If the bomb's weight was inaccurately input by only a few pounds, the bomb could potentially miss the target by thousands of feet, killing innocent civilians or allowing the Japs or Jerries to escape the deadly shockwave.

The aircraft moved across the sky at two hundred miles per hour. This low-level bombing mission at four thousand feet was a tactical maneuver to make it difficult for enemy artillery and menacing flak to accurately be aimed at the bombers. These cadets had not yet been assigned to a particular bomber category and therefore needed to learn how to bomb at all altitudes.

Daniel searched for a visual on the target below across a landscape of vast nothingness. In the distance, the target, a white canvas pyramid, reflected the desert sun. The bomb doors opened as the aircraft neared its prey below. The turbulence increased as the air rushed over the open belly of the plane. Four circles comparable to a dart board surrounded the target. Each circle had been carved into the desert's sand by a large excavator. From this altitude, the target was so small, and the distance was closing faster with each passing second. The release time was critical. Too soon and the bombs would hit before he wanted them to; too long and the bombs would fly right over the outer circle. LaHurd fantasized that the pyramid was a small Japanese airfield. Looking through his sight and making improvised tweaks, he released his armament with an effortless touch of a button. He watched and watched as the bomb fell. Impact! It

---

* Trail is the horizontal distance the bomb is behind the airplane at the instant of impact.

missed by just ninety feet, exploding like a sack of black flour within the second circle. The air force didn't use live bombs during most training missions. It would have been a waste of explosives.

LaHurd's voice shouted over the microphone, "I think I found my niche, boys!"

With the converging factor, his score for the bombing run was 172 feet, and he was damn proud that his first run was nearly sixty points below the curve. In the end, he would make four more runs on the target, holding his average right around 172 feet. The only negative was that since this was his first run with bombs, it was considered a practice mission, and practice missions didn't count as recorded bombs. He'd have to do just as well the next time up.

Fri. Jan. 29, 1943
Deming, New Mexico

Dear Folks

I finally got time to drop you good people a line. They really kept us busy this week. We got up at 5 A.M.—had breakfast at 6 A.M.—down to the flight line at 6:45 A.M.—fly for two hours and hang around for two more—back between 12 + 1 P.M.—eat at 1 P.M.—school 2 P.M. to 5 P.M.—athletics 5:15 to 6:15—eat at 6:45—and trainers from 7:30 to 11:30—bed by 12 A.M. and up again at 5 A.M. Some day. No kidding I was so tired that I'd rather sleep than eat and a couple of times I missed lunch so I could get an extra hour of sleep. We will finish with trainers tomorrow night so next week should be easy. We'll be done at 6:15 P.M. instead 11:30 and that means extra sleep. I had two days of dry runs (dropped no bombs) and one day we went up but the visibility was poor so we returned and yesterday I dropped my first 5 bombs and what a thrill that was. My procedure was poor but that will improve with time. My average error was 90 ft at 4000 ft alt. which is pretty good but the sad part is there is a converging factor of 1.92 that we have to multiply that by, which gives me a score of 172 ft error which is still above average. I hope I can keep it up. Tomorrow I'll probably drop from 1000 ft.

School isn't getting any harder but I had a tough time keeping awake in class and most of the stuff drifted passed me and test coming up tomorrow. I guess I'll have to use my 20-20 vision.

Tell Cal to stay out [of the military] *if he can as he won't like the regular army and he won't be able to get officers training or some other good branch of the service with his vision.*

I'm sorry I let Neils birthday pass without sending him something but I just didn't think of it.

We'll be getting paid tomorrow or Monday and it will come in handy as I'm broke. Not even a copper but don't send me any as I'll get paid before the money reaches me. Haven't much use for money out here anyhow but in your pocket. I owe out $41 and I have $45 owed to me so I'm a little ahead this month. See what no gambling does. When I was gambling I had a surplus now I'm broke.

I won't be going out tomorrow as I have trainer from 7:30 to 11:30 P.M. and anyhow that will give me a chance to catch up on some most needed sleep as we can sleep late on Sundays. Feeling swell in spite of no sleep and doing O.K. so far.

Love + Kisses
Dan

After his first practice run, LaHurd began recording his bombs for Phase I. His average score fluctuated up and down over the circular error benchmark. He dropped bombs from one thousand feet, four thousand feet and eleven thousand feet. His best scores came from the high-altitude bombing runs, potentially deputizing him as a B-17 or B-24 bombardier. For each mission at a new altitude, the cadets were given a practice run with nonrecorded bombs. It seemed as though LaHurd put the armament in proximity to the target on each practice run, but when they really counted, his circular error grew. He wrote home, "When I drop my recorded bombs from up there they go all over the desert."

Sunday Feb. 7, 1943
Deming, New Mexico

Dear Folks
I just got back from the flight Surgeon where I had a recheck on part of my eye test and believe I passed it this time.

We had our usual test yesterday and I believe I passed all three of them, by the skin of my teeth.

This week is the last week in our first phase of bombing. The first phase is day bombing—second phase is night bombing—and third phase is combat bombing. We drop 50 bombs in each phase and I have 15 bombs to go yet to finish my first phase. I really have to put those 15 in there as my circular error is a little above the limit. Anyhow I'm still in the pitching.

Went into town last night and had a tough steak dinner and a beer. Hung around a little while and returned. Nothing to do as usual but to leave the post for a little while makes you feel good. We have to drill today as punishment for throwing papers in the hall. First time since leaving Santa Ana.

The rest of my 15 bombs this coming week will be from 11000 ft. Up there we have to wear oxygen masks plus fur lined jackets and boots (they have the fur lined pants but that makes it too much) plus what we usually have to wear throat mike and ear phones and work the sight. Lets hope I put those 15 in there.

You wanted to know what we had to work on in computers. Well— we had to find—ground speed—wind velocity—drift—direction of the wind—heading—multiply—divide—times + distances and etc. Of course all in different problems. Can't tell you to much, those military men might get mad and this letter wont find you. Secret equipment at this base.

Feeling swell.

Love + Kisses

Dan

LaHurd successfully finished his daylight bombing runs in mid-February and advanced to Phase Two: night missions. He knew that he was really going to have to lower his error ratio in order to stick around. The targets in the night were extremely hard to see. It was like playing darts in a dark room with someone flashing on the lights for only a brief moment. In that flash of light, one had to find the board, aim the dart and throw while standing on a turbulent, moving platform and accounting for a crosswind. If daylight bombing runs were thought to be hard, then night bombing runs were next to impossible. He wrote home, "You need good luck and a good break on your side for this night bombing. The way the targets are lit up is really a joke and you can't see them till you are darn near over them."

It was a difficult series of missions, but LaHurd succeeded. By mid-February, he had dropped twenty bombs at night and decreased his circular error. Finally, Phase Three came. Not only was it the last phase, but it was also the most taxing to complete. He started combat missions with a circular error already twenty points over the benchmark. Combat bombing worked by a hit-or-miss method. The bombardier had a 20-second run on the target—a miniscule amount of time. A multitude of tasks needed to be crammed into that timeframe. The average run on the target for Phase One and Phase Two was 120 seconds, and the cadets considered that window of time to be small. Most of these combat missions ranged in altitude between five hundred and eleven thousand feet, and again, LaHurd excelled in the high-altitude bombing runs.

Toward the end of February and into the beginning of March 1943, LaHurd was faced with another daunting task: boosting his parents' morale. While it was customary for the family back home to write optimistic letters to keep their GI calm, when the military started calling up Daniel's brothers for training, his mother's and father's spirits began to sink.

The military was knocking on Michael's door asking him to serve his country. It was going to be tough for him to leave his wife and son, but if the time came, he wouldn't have a choice. Fortunately, Mike never had to serve overseas. He remained stateside throughout the war.

Only a couple weeks later, the military began seeking Fred and Walt Aboud—Daniel's cousin—for service. And just days after Fred and Walt finished signing papers for service, the military drafted the LaHurd clan's youngest boy. Pa Joe and Mary were stunned when Calvin was finally drafted in early March. Their intelligent and witty son had never expected to be summoned by the government due to his poor vision. During Calvin's childhood, he had been half blinded by a rock slamming into his eye. As time went on, his vision recouped, but never fully. For this reason, he thought it was impossible for the military to draft him and send him overseas. But America needed every fit and capable man in order to continue fighting across the globe.

Daniel wrote home after receiving word that Calvin had been drafted, "I don't want my little brother going to war, that is my job." But by mid-March, Calvin was off to Fort Hayes, and Fred and Walt were packed up for infantry training. Daniel wrote to his father:

> *I really hate to see them go but that's the way things work. It's a real shame the army has to take kids like those boys—never been around much. It must be tough on you and Ma but someday soon we'll all be back and what a party we'll have. Cal will be alright after he meets a few buddies and learns the ropes. It's just like a new job and you have to work awhile to find the easiest way to do it....He'll be a much wiser kid after this is all over.... Fred will be alright and the army will do him good. Tell him to sweat the war out by going to school, don't want to see that kid get hurt.*

Daniel continued bombing runs over Deming. By the end of March, he had ten more bombs to drop and had to deliver direct hits with two of them to complete the training at Deming and ultimately become a second lieutenant. By this date, he had already been issued his personal flight equipment: wool sweater, leather jacket, pair of gloves, gabardine flight suit, pair of wool-lined flight boots, wool-lined jacket and pants, oxygen mask, life preserver, goggles, sunglasses, two bags to put the stuff in, one light and one heavy helmet, parachute and bombardier kit. His brand-new and personally tailored uniform came as well. The military had given him a $250 allowance for the uniform. He was glad to have it because he never would have wanted to pay for the $75 jacket, $25 pants, $18 shirt and other accessories out of his own pocket. He had to admit, though, it was a swell outfit. The ladies were going to go crazy over it.

After receiving these officer luxuries and bombardier necessities, it would have been a shame to fail and give them all back. So LaHurd buckled down and made sure to place as many of his last few bombs as possible on top of the target. His last ten bombs were dropped, and he scored two direct hits, putting him under the benchmark.

March 24, 1943
Deming, New Mexico

Dear Folks

I received a letter from Cal yesterday and today both, and he likes his new home much better than Fort Hayes. I wrote him a three page letter this morning and I also sent him one of my graduation cards yesterday. I'll try to write to him + Fred as much as possible.

One reason I didn't go to El Paso more often was that I couldn't get an overnight pass—too many "gigs."

They've been keeping us pretty busy signing different papers but I believe I've signed the last one just a little bit ago. I signed my discharge paper from the cadets a couple of days ago and after 24 hours after signing, well I'm a civilian again, till Saturday but it doesn't do me any good as I'm still under the iron hand of the army.

I took my navigation flight Monday and did alright—anyhow I returned to my home field. A few times the cadet and myself didn't know where we were but after sitting tight we spotted a landmark that we recognized on the map—so we were O.K. Yesterday morning we went to the machine gun range and fired 100 rounds with a 30 cal. It was fun. I really enjoyed it and I did fairly well considering that was the first machine gun I ever handled. Yesterday I had two missions at 500 feet and completed both of them. Five bombs on each mission and one hit on each mission—that completes my bombs and am I glad. I believe the only thing left to do is a instrument calibration run and that is only for laughs. I got 25 shots at skeet this morning and got seven hits—same as last time—at least I haven't got worse. I didn't do much of anything this noon but I did get enough courage up to go get a haircut. Tonight we are having a dress rehearsal of our officers uniforms and our Squadron Officer is going to inspect us. Gee! are the clothes nice. I wish you could see me graduate but I know it is almost impossible. I know you'll be proud anyway.

I'll never believe I made it till they pin the bars + wings on me. It sure has been tough going sometimes but I managed to stick it out—one of us LaHurds had to be an officer in Uncle Sam's Army.

Keep your chins up.

Feeling swell and hope I'll get to see you soon.

Love + Kisses
Dan

With training over, LaHurd spent his last few days at Deming Air Field firing a shotgun at clay pigeons. He continued to take a class in navigation and studied his Norden Bombsight. But the best news came with the information that his brother Fred had been rejected from the military due to his poor feet.

Monday March 29, 1943
Deming, New Mexico

Dear Folks

I should have written sooner but I was really busy. They had us running like mad. The best news I've had since I've been in the army is when I received your letter telling me that Fred was rejected [from the military]. Boy! that to me was better than receiving my silver wings.

Well Folks, the "Punk is in like Flynn." It was really a thrill and I appreciate it more because I had to work exactly a year for it and hard, but not as hard as I'm going to have to work the next eighteen weeks. We received our orders Saturday right after graduation and I'm one of the 30 fellows going to Hondo, Texas to take a 18-week course in navigation. That's what I get for getting a good grade in the navigation course here. I'm really going to be educated after the army gets through with me. The best part of that is I'll be drawing $246 a month (really $291 but they take out for the room) but I have to buy my own meals now. Not bad pay for going to school. I'll give you an idea how the gang was split—30 to Hondo

Texas—21 instructors—some to a tart outfit—and the others are going to get a five week course in navigation and go into light bombardment B-26 B-25 A-20 low altitude—me I'm slated for high altitude and the higher the better for me. I won't see action probably for eight months that is if I get through the navigation course alright—if not they'll probably make a mess officer out of me. I can't lose—the army is paying for it.

I really think I got a good deal when I got this navigation deal because if I get through that I'll really have something that is worth while. It is really going to be rugged—all we'll be down there is glorified cadets but hell I can stand five more months I've stood it this long.

We had open post from Saturday noon till 8 A.M. Monday and what a time we had. We went to Silver City about 60 miles west of Deming and really raised hell. They have a girls school there and we had the best lookers there. We really operated. We didn't get back till Monday morning around 7 A.M. and that is why I missed your call Sunday. I tried calling several times today but couldn't do any good. I'll try again early tomorrow morning. I hope you weren't worried about me, as I'm feeling swell.

The custom is to send your best girlfriend the wings that are issued to you so tell Ma just as soon as I find a little box I'm sending her mine and I want her to wear them always.

Oh! I almost forgot to mention that we leave for Texas tomorrow night or Wed. morning. Little by little I'm getting closer to home or am I. I'm sorry to say no furlough this time so I guess we'll have to sweat out another five months. I'm bound to get one sometime—that is if they ever quit sending me to school!

How's the Cal the "Babe"?

I'll let you know my new address as soon as I know.

Pa, you can quit sending the Beacon *to me as I won't have time to read it anymore. Transfer it to Cal.*

Boy!! do these officers uniforms look sharp and you can really operate in them. I am now an officer + a gentleman but it took an act of Congress to make me a gentleman.

Love + Kisses
Daniel E. LaHurd 2nd Lt A.

Fred's rejection from the military couldn't have made Daniel and his parents happier. Fred, on the other hand, was absolutely crushed. He was upset and demoralized that while his brothers and friends were preparing to fight and defend the United States, he was now forced to stay home and work as a civilian.

Top: Katz's Klassy Klip Klub, February 19, 1943.

Left: Calvin LaHurd poses just months after being drafted into the military.

Left: Daniel poses in his heavy, wool-lined coat, parachute harness and communication headset at Deming.

Right: *From left to right*: Vincent Ginks Ginkus from Glenwood, Illinois; Joseph P. Horvantz from Cleveland, Ohio; and Daniel E. LaHurd from Akron, Ohio. Here the men are dressed in their new officers' uniforms after graduating from Deming's bombardier training.

Daniel's parents now had to cope with two sons and a nephew in the military while the war overseas escalated. Time would tell where and how their boys would fight the war, but Joseph and Mary knew that their sons' days in the United States were ending.

LaHurd would find himself in Hondo, Texas, training in navigational tactics during the spring and summer of 1943. The good news for Daniel was that Ginks was also heading there. The bad news was that he had actually enjoyed being a bombardier so much and feared that if he did a good job in Texas, he'd become a navigator instead.

Chapter 6

FLYING BOOKKEEPERS

April 1, 1943–August 1, 1943

Anyone who fights, even with the most modern weapons, against an enemy who
dominates the air, is like a primitive warrior who stands against modern forces,
with the same limitations and the same chance of success.
—Field Marshal Erwin Rommel

Pa Joe, the dark-eyed businessman wearing suspenders and a brown top
hat, walked through the door of his home after a long and hard day's
work. The conservatively dressed father of five hung his hat just inside the
door to reveal his thick gray head of hair. At fifty-three, Pa Joe was known
in the city as an extremely quiet and serious man. His silence would only
deepen through these war days. Emotional fatigue was obvious from the
bluish circles surrounding his eyes. His thin wire glasses did little to hide
the always-present emotions and worrisome thoughts of his sons' absence
from home. He wished things could return to the way they were; Sunday
afternoon meals and gatherings, Saturdays devoted to the horse tracks and
evenings spent sitting on the porch with his boys. Calvin, Daniel and his
nephew Walt were each off training for war. For Pa Joe, the past weeks
had been and continued to be extremely difficult to bear. The odds of
one son going off to war and surviving was bad enough; two sons and a
nephew going off to war seemed a great temptation to fate. He wondered
if he'd ever experience those good days again. The war had already taken
so many young lives, and Joseph prayed that his boys wouldn't become
part of the daunting statistics that filled the newspapers.

Daniel had written home to his father weeks earlier: "Pa, never worry about us—in case something ever does happen to us—you will hear quick enough and know that I love you and Ma."

Relieving the muscles in his arm, he rested a brown paper bag holding meatless foods—rationed flour, honey, beans, unsliced bread, potatoes and a few eggs—on the oak dining room table. While the war continued to progress overseas, the LaHurds and many other Americans were forced to change their way of life at home. Cooking ingredients like sugar, canned foods and eggs were stringently rationed by the government. For the LaHurds, Mondays, Wednesdays and Fridays became meatless days when the family prepared their meals with wheat, fruits and vegetables. Many other families across the nation did the same. Many women found this difficult at the outset. Growing up, they had learned to cook traditional cuisine from family recipes. Vegetarian meals were unheard of. Families had to figure out new ways to eat. Macaroni and cheese replaced meat. Honey or molasses became a popular substitute for sugar in baked goods. To Mary, it was all worth the extra trouble, and she contributed in any way to assist the young boys fighting overseas.

The LaHurds and many other Americans had more money in their pockets today in comparison to the days of the Great Depression; the war had created millions of new jobs. U.S. citizens found themselves with greater spending power; however, they knew their frugality was critical to the war effort. Americans' obedience to rationing laws was paramount. Consumers economized on goods and services, recycled waste and scrap, planted Victory Gardens, canned vegetables, complied with price controls and rationing laws and put discretionary income into war bonds.

Every American's life was touched by this war in some way. The government was curtailing and even halting the production of many popular goods—cars, bicycles, electrical appliances, batteries, metal household furniture, metal household utensils, razors, toys, vacuum cleaners and even metal caskets. Metal would be used to produce bullets, tanks, aircraft, ships and other war materials.

Many small businesses across the country, now unable to produce and sell their specialized goods to the public, were revamping their business strategies and transforming their companies' outputs. Industries that were once building merry-go-rounds, musical instruments, pinball machines, tissues, orange juice squeezers or caskets were now building gun mounts, plane gears, airplane parts, 20mm shell cases, armor piercing shells, .50-caliber machine gun mounts, bullet molds and aircraft. One pound of fat contained enough glycerin to make a pound of black powder; thirty thousand razor blades contained enough steel to make fifty .30-caliber machine guns; 2,300 pairs of nylon stockings went into one parachute; and thirty lipstick tubes contained enough brass to make twenty cartridges.

Because of rationing and the government freeze placed on the manufacturing of discretionary goods, Americans had to find other ways to spend their dollars. One popular release that dipped into America's wallet was betting on the horse races. Annual bets at the horse tracks nearly doubled from 1943 to 1944, and Joseph LaHurd, much to his wife's displeasure, was a huge contributor to that increase. Just as Daniel was able to mentally distance himself from the stresses of war through poker, the horse tracks assuaged Pa Joe's fears of his sons' absence from home.

Mary stuck her head out of the kitchen, where she had been preparing dinner, to greet her husband and collect a few of the necessary ingredients from the half-full grocery bag that he had carried from the store. Looking at Joe with hope, she always asked him the same question at his arrival: "Are there any letters from our beautiful boys?"

His response with a slight grin was always, "I've missed you too. And yes, there are letters."

After slipping off his shoes, he pulled out a stack of creased and stained envelopes dated over the past two weeks. Days' worth of information about Daniel and Calvin sat on the dining room table. This moment became the high point of Joseph and Mary's day.

Mary untied her white apron, stained with tomato juice, and scurried over to the table where her husband sat. With the unopened envelopes on the table, the house seemed suspended in an eerie quiet. Joe and Mary's love for each other never faltered during this time of stress, depression and chaos, but this unnatural silence seemed to be a common occurrence. Often they just sat and contemplated where their sons were. What were they doing right now? Where would they be deployed overseas? Many hours were spent in silent prayer.

Over one year had passed since Daniel had traveled away on the troop train. The only communication up to this point was through letters and a few telephone calls. Joseph and Mary knew full well what was going on in the world. They knew what Hitler was capable of, they knew what the Japanese were willing to do to win and they knew what the American soldier was facing on a daily basis in Europe, Africa and the Pacific. The newspapers and radio waves told stories of all the soldiers departing for battle. The headlines were full of the names of local men and boys who were missing or had been killed in action. Pa Joe and Mary understood what their sons were preparing for, and they tried to prepare themselves every day for the news that would soon come, informing them that Daniel or Calvin or Walt had been shipped across either the Pacific or the Atlantic to fight.

A three-cent postage stamp filled the top right corner of each envelope, and the return address read Hondo Air Field. Only forty miles west of San Antonio and three miles from Hondo, Texas, the airfield had been built in less than ninety days at a cost of $7.25 million. This colossal base occupied over 3,600 Texas acres, making it the largest navigation training facility in the world.

Between July 1942 and August 1945, some 14,158 men were trained in navigation at Hondo. The aspiring airmen used B-34s, B-18s, AT-7s and AT-11s to learn the art of navigation. Their primary responsibility was to direct the flight from departure to destination and return, with an emphasis on return. The airmen who were schooled here called themselves the "Flying Bookkeepers." The navigator was known to be the busiest man on the plane. He was occupied with his instruments, charts and compass from the time the aircraft left the ground until the time the aircraft landed.

At Hondo, the airmen were taught the art of geographic positioning and focused on the four means of navigation: pilotage, dead reckoning, radio and celestial. The future navigators needed to know each technique and employ it based on the situation. They used pilotage when a visual of the ground below was not obstructed by fog, clouds or darkness. With pilotage, the plane was directed by known visual references like natural or architectural landmarks. When the view of the earth below was obstructed, the navigators resorted to dead reckoning or radio navigation. Dead reckoning determined the position of the aircraft by keeping an account of the track and distance flown over the earth's surface from the point of departure or last known position. Radio navigation employed various radio aids to determine where the bomber was at any given time. The most difficult technique to learn was the science of celestial navigation, which used referencing of two or more celestial bodies.

Daniel had been at the airfield for two weeks now and was settling in to yet another base. The scenery was not much different than Deming. Instead of battling sand in their bunks, the airmen combated Texas ants. Any food brought to the barracks was a magnet for the pesky insects. This created countless sleepless nights for the airmen as they shared quarters with their uninvited sleeping partners.

The main distinction between Hondo and Deming was the degree of freedom and level of respect that LaHurd and the other officers received. The base was made up of commissioned officers and noncommissioned airmen. All noncomms were required to salute their superiors. LaHurd, now an officer, only had to salute other second lieutenants and officers of greater rank. Open post was granted to the officers. After completing their daily duties, they were free to do what they pleased at the base or outside the base, as long as they reported back for duty by 7:00 a.m. the next morning. LaHurd no longer had to worry about obtaining weekend passes because Saturday and Sunday were also open post.

He enjoyed his new life as an officer and all the perks that came with it. Ginks and LaHurd frequented San Antonio on the weekends wearing their brand-new officer uniforms. At other times, Ginks gave LaHurd golf lessons at the driving range. Sometimes the two simply hung around Hondo's officers' club. The club offered beer, liquor and food for a small price. In addition to alcohol and food, the officers' club was a place to sit around and chat, play cards and shoot pool. LaHurd and Ginks quickly formed a pack of new friends. After two weeks at navigation training, they were visiting San Antonio not just as a pair anymore but as part of a small crowd.

Of course, LaHurd was back at it again, chasing the women. For him, it was another town but the same game. He wrote to his parents, "Well I went to town again this weekend and had another swell time. I met a cute dish but she doesn't have an oil well—I'll keep looking for one though. There's only one trouble with these Texas women, they're either too tall or I'm too short—I'll keep looking till I can find one I can kiss without standing on a chair."

LaHurd soon found a keeper. Unfortunately, she didn't possess an oil well, but she did have an affluent family. Her father was a bigwig Texas politician.

LaHurd's prodigal spending, rash gambling and lavish nights with a plethora of women were in part driven by what he knew lay ahead for him. Young Americans were losing their lives on battlefields across the world. The casualty rate was growing faster than an army of Texas ants on leftover candy. Men whom LaHurd had met at Santa Ana and boys he had known from childhood had been shipped overseas to fight for freedom and returned in body bags. He knew that he was soon going to have to face what so many had faced before him. He decided to live for the now because there may not be a now tomorrow. LaHurd understood that he may be living out his last weeks on this planet, and he was determined to have as much fun as possible.

Sitting at the kitchen table, Joseph opened each of the envelopes in succession according to their postage date and read aloud the letter's contents to his wife. Mary sat captivated at the edge of her seat. The letters made her feel good. They alleviated her fears and her motherly worries. Her son was always so positive and jovial with his written words, but she could still sense his underlying emotions. Daniel had written the first letter to Calvin. After Calvin had read it, he sealed it back up and mailed it home. The other letters had been written by Daniel directly to his parents.

April 16, 1943
Hondo, Texas

Dear Cal

I've been pretty busy going to school and then to night study hall every night this week. Why I had to go to night study hall? Well it was this way—15 guys out of 38 passed the test we had last Friday, so the ones that flunked had to go to study hall from 8 P.M. Monday till 9:30 P.M. through Friday. We had another test today + I believe I passed this one as I was getting sick of night study classes—so I really tried. We had a navigation trip yesterday and I had the last leg. We had pilot, instructor and three student officers and each student officer takes a leg. Hondo to Gatesville to Jerk Water Town to Hondo. The total trip was about 700 miles. I had the important one though—I had to find home and glory be! I did—only eight miles off course but you could easily see the field eight miles away. I really got sick up there and let my stomach come up about five times. You can imagine what came up the fifth time—nothing, but I really did think I was going to toss up my intestines. I wish I had, maybe I could have gottin out of the army.

Well! Babe! I'm going into town tomorrow and knock myself out again. Gee! I wish you were here—no kidding, we could have a good time together.

You talk about guard duty—when I had it at Santa Ana, we were on for 24 hours 2 on four off.

Thanks Cal but I don't need any cash yet. My buddy + I got pretty lucky a couple of nights ago and made us $52, enough for this weekend but Cal if you need anything—money—clothes—anything at all let me know and I'll beg—borrow or steal but you'll get it pronto.

Cal I wouldn't take a chance of going home on a 3 day pass—Boy! if you're late returning they'll really rack you back plenty so be careful. If I ever get a chance I'll try and take a run up there. Who knows you might get transferred near here after you finish your basic training.

I've been getting some golf lessons from my side kick "The Gink"—he was champ of Chicago and he sure is a swell golfer and a hellava swell guy.

I received your letter today with your picture in it and to tell you the truth it was lousy. I'd have some good snapshots taken or a good picture—those dime shots always make one look lousy. You should have seen some I had taken—tore them up before I looked at them twice. I'll send you some snapshots I had taken as soon as I get them developed. Don't forget send me a good picture.

Hey! how do you like the army by now?

Well kid I'm running out of words so I'll close for now.

Love

Dan

P.S. Listen Cal, always have a good time when you go into town and on the field. No kidding I sometimes have a better time in the barracks bullshitting than what I have in town.

April 16, 1943

Hondo, Texas

Dear Folks

Just a few lines to let you know I'm O.K. and still in there pitching. We had our first navigation flight yesterday and I got sicker than a dog with fits, but I still brought the plane home O.K. and was only 1 minute off on my ETA (estimated time of arrival) although I was eight miles off course and knew it but I was to sick to make a correction so I let it go. We had another test today and think I passed it. I had a problem sheet that was blank on one side and didn't know there was suppose to be problems on it so I lost 11 points right there but I still think I passed it. If not I'll raise hell and see if I can get credit for it.

I received a letter from Walt + Cal today and I think I'll be able to write to the Babe tonight. I'm glad Fred got a job, now you'll be able to payoff the house quick, what, say, we all pitch in and pay it off this year. I'll do my share.

I'm all set to go into town tomorrow and maybe play a game of golf and other things. I ordered a couple of more sun tan shirts and one pants last Saturday and it set me back $40—Boy! are officers cloths expensive. $12.50 for shirt—$15 for pants and they're tailored—nice but expensive. They'll be finished at the end of the month—payday time.

I met Tony Testa in San Antonio yesterday. He's stationed at San Marcos, Texas about 70 miles from here. I hadn't seen him since I left for primary and had to run into him here. It sure is a small world.

Well that's all for now.

Feeling swell.

Love + Kisses

Dan

———

April 27, 1943

Hondo, Texas

Dear Folks

I finally bought some stationary. I was getting pretty tired of using the Gunter Hotel paper and so were they.

Well! I fooled them in this last test that we had Friday and passed with an 83%—better than I expected and I believe I did pretty well in the mission that I flew yesterday. I'm getting closer to destination—I was only 6 miles right of course and my ETA was right on the nose.

I'm sorry I didn't send an Easter greeting but I really didn't think—first place—it didn't seem like Easter to me—second place—I really didn't know it was Easter creeping up so soon. Ah! yes—I went to church. Proud of me now?

Cal's having quite a time at Fort Riley—Gee! he's having a better time than I am. Playing ball + all. How could he send $40 home. I best take lessons from him on how to save on army pay. He really is tops.

Well! Pa getting down to the serious side—I'll start by answering some questions.

1. There is no place where Ma could get a room here in Hondo. She would have to stay in a Hotel in San Antonio and that is too expensive.

2. They have busses from S. Antonio to Hondo but I don't know of any other place they come from.

3. I really believe that I'll get a furlough after finishing here and that isn't so long as time is going pretty fast. Here I'm in my 4th week already.

The best thing to do is wait till I get my furlough as I wouldn't want Ma to come down here alone. The trip would just about kill her. The trains are overcrowded and it's no fun for civilians to travel by train. There are no rooms available in San Antonio except hotels. The married soldiers have them all pretty well tied up. I really would like to see you but the expense would be terrific. The hotel bill at $3 a day for a month *plus food + train fare—it's really not worth the trouble + expense. Save the money and we'll throw a big party when I get home. Cal + I should get one about the same time.*

Well everything is coming along swell and I'm feeling sweller than swell. I sure hope you had a nice EASTER.

Love + Kisses
Dan

By the time Joseph finished reading the letters, Mary had relaxed back into her chair. Her hand was softly holding her husband's. No bad news. Her son seemed to be safe. His spirits seemed to be high. From what she had heard, Daniel was at a good base, enjoying his off time, growing friendships and staying out of trouble. Pa Joe was happy to hear that Daniel was earning good money, working hard and enjoying more freedom as an officer.

Daniel was flying more frequently week over week. He continued to battle airsickness that had first appeared at Sequoia Field and had followed him through Deming to Hondo. He wrote to his parents about his airsickness: "I was hoping the plane would crash and put me out of my misery—that's the way we all feel when we get airsick." He joked that the sickness was a sign from God that he should have joined the infantry. The feeling was so unbearable at times that he would simply give up his navigation duties, forcing the instructor to get the crew back to base.

Each gruelingly long flight was broken into multi-leg stints. Destination points were from Texas city to Texas city. Oftentimes, the aircraft traveled five hundred to seven hundred miles, with trips lasting as long as six exhausting hours. The student navigator received a grade for each of the typical three legs and was given aggregate grades for each phase: pilotage, dead reckoning, instruments and celestial.

LaHurd quickly found navigation to be dry and uneventful. The position just didn't have the same appeal as a bombardier. There was no climactic point in the mission. There was no excitement during the long flights. He wrote a letter to Calvin explaining his dislike for the job:

May 18, 1943
Hondo, Texas

Dear Cal
Just a note to let you know I haven't forgotten you. Well! handsome I still am doing my best to try to like navigation but so far I haven't succeeded. I did pretty well in my last two missions and got an 88% in the last test. In

fact, I'm doing too good to suit me—I shouldn't do so good—than I'd get washed out and life would become interesting again. Boy! are these AT–7's cracking up. Five guys hit the silk two weeks ago—five Sunday—and five today. One good thing the chutes work. They've grounded all the AT–7's for a while—till they find what's causing the trouble—probably mostly pilots head up his ass. Don't tell the folks this.

Hey! what's this about you wanting to send me something—don't be foolish—I'm making five times as much as you and if anybody is going to do any sending it will be me. Thanks anyhow Cal. I got all the clothes and other things I can use—in fact I have so many I sent some home to be stored.

Hey! Cal, have you run across any good looking chicks. Listen—don't be particular in the army any babe will do till something better comes along. Cal can you use a brass buckle?—if you can I'll send you one. Have you low cut dress shoes? Give me an idea what you need to help give you that sharp appearance when you go out.

Inclosing a letter Walt sent to Fred—Pa sent to me—Me to you. O.K. Well! that's all for now—be good—and have a good time.

Love
Dan

LaHurd wasn't fond of the continuous stresses created by intricate charting from takeoff to landing, and he missed the action and quick thrill of being a bombardier. He wanted to get back to high-altitude bombing. It had been such a thrill when he dropped real bombs from the AT-11. Daniel wrote to his family, "I'm really afraid I'm going to get through this [navigation] course and if I do I'll be a navigator sure as Christ made green apples. I'll have to forget I ever was a bombardier and that's my first love."

As spring turned to summer, Daniel debated with himself whether to purposely wash out of navigation so that he could go back to being a bombardier. While he was training over the badlands of Texas, his younger brother was becoming an infantryman for the U.S. Army.

Calvin's training had been anything but easy. He had heard more swear words and seen more spit fly from his superiors' mouths during his eight weeks of basic training than he had hoped to hear and see in an entire lifetime. He had put up with the onerous tasks and malicious rhetoric of basic training. After basic, he was unhappy to be working in the Small Arms Department, running around and loading machine gun belts and throwing cases of bullets on range trucks at Fort Riley. He wrote to Daniel, "This job is a job made for a slave."

With Calvin in the service, Daniel's outgoing correspondence began to slant more toward Fort Riley, Kansas, and less toward Akron, Ohio. The letters coming from Hondo helped boost Calvin's morale and also came with advice on how to make military life a bit easier. And a bit easier went a long way. Daniel knew it was important to keep Calvin's spirits high and felt he could be of some inspiration to his little brother. Daniel wrote to Calvin:

> *Hi you old sharpshooter—so you got yourself a medal—Boy! I'm really proud of ya. Keep up the good work and let's get one for the machine gun. Cal I sent you three pounds of candy and a pound of nuts Saturday and I hope you enjoy it. Have a good time with the ten bucks—that's for winning a medal—I'll make it $20 for the machine gun—Is it a deal?*

Daniel had made up his mind that navigation wasn't what he wanted to do. He decided to wash out of the course, purposefully failing his navigation missions. He was determined to become a bombardier. Why not? He was good at it, he enjoyed it and the position's responsibility lasted minutes rather than hours. At the end of July 1943, he wrote home, "I can navigate a plane with the best in my class. They wanted to give me a dead reckoning rating but I refused it. Too good of a chance of getting a medium bomber with that rating." As a result, Daniel was finally washed out of navigation.

After nearly a year and a half away from home, just as the military was giving him reassignment orders, LaHurd was finally offered a two-week furlough home. Unbeknownst to him, this trip would change his life forever.

Chapter 7

ROSES AND RIVETS

August 2, 1943–August 16, 1943

One front and one battle where everyone in the United States, every man, woman, and child—is in action. That front is right here at home, in our daily lives.
—President Franklin Roosevelt

Daniel's mother barely recognized her son as he walked through the front door of 1099 Berwin Street in his crisp chocolate-colored officer's uniform topped by a precisely creased hat. Daniel had matured over the past year. He possessed a toughness that was unseen in the past. He was toned but thinner than she remembered. His olive skin, darkened by the Texas sun, made him look robust, and his clean military shave added to the appearance of perfection. But most important, his winsome smile proved that his charm and charismatic personality hadn't succumbed to the rigors of military training.

Mary's mood instantly transformed from melancholy to pure joy. She wrapped her arms around her son and squeezed as she whispered a prayer. His absence had been too long, and Mary hated being away from her children for such lengthy intervals of time. She kept smiling. Leading Daniel into the kitchen, she jokingly scolded him with slightly broken English, "You are not eating enough. Those soldiers don't feed you right. They just can't. You're all skin and bones, honey."

Daniel explained the reason for his slim build. "They run us like mad. We are constantly doing something: marching, cross-country runs, calisthenics, lifting and moving stuff, you name it. And they don't cook food like you,

Ma." Grinning, he added, "And God knows it isn't easy chasing around those beautiful Texas women all weekend long."

The heels of Daniel's polished dress shoes tapped on the hall's oak hardwood floor as Mary led her son into the kitchen.

"Well, I have a couple weeks to fatten you up a bit. And you better watch yourself with those ladies," his mother said fondly. She practically floated around the kitchen as she prepared lunch for Daniel, humming a faint melody as she prepared a sandwich and sliced a few carrots.

Daniel had a lot of questions for his mother. He wanted to know about last Christmas, Easter and the beginning of summer that had been filled with birthdays. He wanted to know how his mother had spent the twenty dollars he had sent home to her for Mother's Day.* He wanted to know how his little nieces and nephew were doing in school. He wanted to know how the neighborhood was holding up. He wanted to know how she was holding up. They sat at the kitchen table for the entire afternoon as she answered all of his questions.

Mary was glad to speak about home. She didn't want to hear stories of training or to gain inside information about the war. Those questions would come as soon as Mike, Fred and Pa Joe came home from work. At the moment, she only wanted to feed her son, answer his questions and hold his hand.

That evening, the entire family gathered at Joseph and Mary's home for dinner. It was superb, almost like the good old days before the war. Calvin had managed to make it home too. The family was ecstatic to have their military boys back at home. Pa Joe and Mary just sat and smiled throughout the entire dinner. Mike, Fred, Calvin and Daniel joked and laughed together. Louise asked hundreds of questions and chronicled the town's gossip from the past year. Neil, Mary Lou and Linda Lou divided time between one another to sit on Uncle Dan's lap. He had such an extraordinary time that he actually found it difficult to finish the night and head to bed. He simply couldn't wait for the war to be over so he could return to this decent life.

Much of Daniel's furlough was spent helping his mother around the house, relaxing and visiting family. The majority of his friends around town had been drafted or had volunteered for service over the past year. This eliminated any chance of playing cards or going out for drinks. The boys who had not been grabbed by Uncle Sam were working hard in the factories building equipment for war.

---

* The spending power of $20 in 1943 would be equal to nearly $250 today.

His second day home, an early Saturday morning, he and Calvin walked to one of their father's grocery stores to visit their dad. Maybe some muscle was needed around the storage room. On their walk over, they noticed that their hometown had changed drastically over the prior year. Everyone appeared busier than before. The foot traffic was heavy, but the street was virtually free of automobiles. It was amazing how the war had already touched every aspect of the neighborhood and the city.

Daniel and Calvin made their way to a storefront where a sign hanging over the door read "LaHurd's Grocery, A Modern Square Deal Store" in bold black letters across a clean white background. The store was wedged tightly between an apartment building and an authentic Italian restaurant. Rationing signs hung in the pristine windows. An American flag and an army flag dangled from either side of the building. As the front door opened, a chiming brass bell alerted Joseph that a customer was present. The aromas of bread, spices, fresh fruits and vegetables hit the boys' nostrils. Their father looked up from behind the meat counter, where he was slicing rationings of beef for his customers. Meat had become a seriously depleted commodity. Citizens often traveled from store to store in search of it. Joseph did his best to keep his stores stocked with this valuable source of protein.

A big smile crossed Pa Joe's face when he saw his sons. "Hey boys, come on over here and help an old man cut some meat," he called across the store.

The inside was immaculate. Everything had its place. Daniel and Calvin joined their father behind the counter. Each put on a spare apron and started to chop away, stopping periodically to wrap small portions of marbled beef or poultry in white packing paper. The boys and their father chatted with the customers, charmed the women, handed out candy to the children and joked with the men.

Joseph was closely acquainted with many of his customers. Most of his shoppers were aware that Daniel and Calvin were in training and would soon be sent overseas. Thus, most of the conversation as the customers waited for their meat was centered on war and training. Many wanted to know what it was like to fly or shoot machine guns. How fast did the planes travel? How loud were the guns? How high could the planes really go? What does it look like from way up there?

Daniel alternated between his slicing knife, trimming the fat from the red meat, and his cleaver, hacking through larger pieces of meat on the bone, as he tried to answer questions from curious customers. Most were fascinated when Daniel explained the power of the bombers' engines. Others cared more about where he'd traveled to and what he'd seen. Calvin wrapped chunks of meat in white packing paper and joked with customers. He talked about the guns he had fired, rigorous boot camp and where he had traveled. Daniel and Calvin enjoyed the attention. Best of all, they could see that their father was proud, making all their training worth it.

As Daniel sharpened his slicing knife, the tiny bell at the front door dinged just as it had all morning. This time, a stunning young lady entered. Her dazzling appearance hit Daniel like a ton of bricks. She looked familiar, but Daniel couldn't place a name to the beautiful face. Her powdered skin sent chills down the young airman's spine. Her stunning blonde hair, classy style and independent attitude made his entire body tense up. A debutant and confident woman, she personified strength, looking like Rosy the Riveter herself had walked out of a propaganda poster.

She glanced over at the men behind the meat counter and grinned as Daniel and Calvin stared, jaws dropped. Daniel tapped his father on the arm, his eyes never leaving the young lady, and wiggled his bushy eyebrows up and down. His father gestured toward the young woman, who was now walking through an aisle, and shrugged as if to say, "Go ahead, go talk to her."

Pa Joe grabbed his son's elbow and whispered, "Her name is Madeline. Her parents are friends of the family."

Daniel looked over at his brother, winked and said, "Don't even think about it. She's mine. Wish me luck."

He stabbed his thin knife into a piece of meat, hammered his heavy rectangular knife into the scratched and scarred wooden chopping block, washed his hands, fixed his hair and made his way over to the customer. The aisle where she stood shopping was lined with five-foot shelves holding canned foods on either side. Daniel introduced himself and gallantly offered to help her with her grocery basket. She smiled, introduced herself and accepted the offer. As she handed over her basket, her hand grazed Daniel's, and again the chills shot up his back. Pa Joe and Calvin stood on their tippy-toes from behind the counter, peeking over the displays to watch his progress.

The doorbell rang off and on as customers entered and departed. Madeline walked around the store shopping and talking with Daniel for nearly a full hour. He held her grocery basket and followed her around the store, flirting and joking. When she had finished, Daniel personally cashed her out. Before handing over her change, he made her promise him a date later in the afternoon. She accepted with a beaming smile.

Since she was a young girl, Madeline, her five sisters and brother had to provide for her family just like her parents. She was raised as a hard worker and carried that discipline through her teens and into her twenties. Her first job was making artificial fishing lures at Pflueger's Tackle in Akron. When the war started, she obtained a second position working at Goodyear Aircraft. Her long days consisted of working from 7:00 a.m. to 1:00 p.m. at Pflueger's and then taking the streetcar to the Goodyear AirDock, where she worked from 1:30 p.m. to 7:30 p.m. She was a riveter, building Corsair Fighter Planes inside a building that seemed as big as the city itself. Employees there pumped out some of the best war materials in the country underneath the AirDock's massive ceiling.

Her first official date with Daniel was in front of the big screen when they watched Sam Wood's *For Whom the Bell Tolls*, avoiding all the 1943 war movies like *Bataan*, *Combat America*, *Air Force*, *Mission to Moscow* and *Guadalcanal Diary*. Daniel didn't think it possible, but Madeline looked even more beautiful than she had earlier in the day at the grocery store. After leaving the theater, the couple walked only a short distance before finding a vacant wooden bench on Main Street where they sat and relaxed in the late summer afternoon. A newspaper, someone's already read trash, sat on the ground next to them, flapping in the breeze. The front page, headlined "Russian Offensive Smashing Ahead," informed the reader of earlier battles. The bottom of the front page urged everyone to "Purchase War Bonds and Stamps." People lingered, spending their weekend in recreation and freedom. Daniel wondered what the soldiers overseas were experiencing at this very moment: earth-shattering explosions, torture, wounded cries for help, the stench of blood or the search for missing limbs. As much as he wanted this furlough, he could barely stand the thought of sitting on a bench with a beautiful woman while boys were fighting far from home. He stared off into the horizon, thinking of his brother Calvin. Closing his eyes for a brief moment, he shook his head and whispered to himself, "God, I hope nothing happens to my little brother."

Madeline crossed her legs, and Daniel's attention was drawn to her smooth skin. A line chalked down the back of her calf traveled up her thigh until it disappeared underneath her dress. Throughout the war, women drew hose lines with mascara to simulate the appearance that their legs were covered in nylon or silk hose.

The sky above them was Caribbean blue with only a pair of fluffy white clouds tumbling across the late afternoon sky. The red-bricked street wasn't as crammed with taxis, streetcars and buses as Daniel had remembered. Only a few years earlier, the streets of downtown Akron had been packed. After President Roosevelt limited consumers' consumption of gasoline to only a few gallons a week, the average automobile owner curtailed driving. The government's national ban on pleasure driving and a thirty-five-mile-per-hour speed limit on all the nation's highways saved gasoline that could then be used overseas and also increased the longevity of the rubber tires on the vehicles. Rubber was needed on the front lines.

Propaganda posters filled the windows of Main Street's shops. Each advertisement contained a unique picture and catchy phrase: Uncle Sam pointed with his index finger, "I Want You for the U.S. Army"; a clean plate and empty glass on a kitchen table, "Food Is a Weapon, Don't Waste It!"; a woman feeding a soldier's machine gun with aluminum cans, "Save Your Cans: Help Pass the Ammunition"; and an American worker holding up a Bond Certificate, "Wanted—Fighting Dollars."

Something happened while Daniel and Madeline talked comfortably over the sounds of the city. Daniel began to fall for her. He realized that someone special was sitting next to him. She was different from the other girls he had run around with, level headed and strong. As he sat there and opened up to her, realizing that she was fixed on every word, his previously sealed emotions began to spill out. Wanting to spare his parents candid talk about his fears and upcoming battles, Daniel found it easier to open up to Madeline instead. She seemed like someone who could deal with conversations concerning these weighty matters. He needed someone like her. He told stories of nerve-racking training missions and dusty, sandy barracks where men had to lift their sheets before lying down to make sure poisonous spiders or scorpions were not looking for a sleeping partner. He spoke of the lack of sleep; the long, physically torturous days of running and marching; and the fears of his unknown future. He feared that someday soon he might be shipped overseas, never to return home from battle alive. It was this last comment that brought tears to Madeline's eyes: the thought of him never returning to the United States, never marrying or creating a family. Daniel's commanders instilled this real possibility of death into the mind of every officer. Their chances of survival were slim, very slim, and the military wanted its men to understand this. Daniel understood, but the thought still disturbed him.

Madeline, too, was frightened of many things during this confusing time, but talking to Daniel seemed to calm her nerves and anxieties. She realized that she could seek strength and confidence through Daniel,

Daniel poses for a picture while on his furlough home in Akron, Ohio.

and he found that their discussions assuaged his own fears of war.

He looked over at her. A stray piece of blonde hair blew across the front of her face, and her blue eyes seemed to twinkle in the waning sunlight. He wondered if he'd survive the war to come back to this beautiful woman.

She looked at him. He placed his arm behind her back and, with his strong hand, delicately squeezed her shoulder. He smiled, she blushed and they moved closer. They kissed. For a brief moment, as their lips touched, the city sounds, passing pedestrians and thoughts of war slipped away.

As their lips moved apart, Daniel held onto Madeline's shoulder, his passionate grip never easing. They remained close, and for a few seconds, they just stared into each other's eyes. He would never forget this moment.

Chapter 8

GROOM DEPLOYS

August 17, 1943–March 5, 1944

The Navy can lose us the war, but only the Air Force can win it. The fighters are our salvation, but the bombers alone provide the means of victory.
—*Prime Minister Winston Churchill*

Daniel's furlough finally came to an end as he and Calvin were summoned to return to the military. It was time to make his way back to Texas. The trip had been eventful. His mother and father's mood had risen exponentially due to their boys' visit home. And he had fallen in love over the past two weeks. He couldn't believe it, but he was in love with Madeline. His feelings for her only made his trip back to Texas more difficult. The family reunion was over. It was time for the boys to get back to business and train for war.

For a few lazy weeks in Texas, Daniel awaited reassignment orders. His days were over at Hondo. He had washed out of navigation school. Things had swiftly changed during his two-week absence. Ginks had washed out as a Flying Bookkeeper, been reassigned as bombardier and sent to Tampa, Florida. Other friends left for Ohio, Wyoming, Kansas, California and Georgia.

By mid-September, LaHurd's orders took him to Pyote, Texas, where he and eight others banded into a unified crew. Their aircraft was the B-17 bomber. Each crew member's life would soon be in the others' hands. Each man would be responsible for a critical piece of the imminent missions over hostile territory. The men would only have one another on their long and treacherous assignments. Once their bomber left the ground and engaged the enemy at twenty-five thousand feet, there would be no possibility of withdrawal, no medics to tend their wounds, no foxholes to take cover in, no superiors to alter their plan and no time for reinforcements to be called in. Each man would learn to know the importance of his mission and complete that mission at any and all costs. The crew, and the crew alone, would be manning empty guns, assisting in navigation and the recognition of hostiles and collectively improvising as problems arose.

Fred Wickham from Baltimore, Maryland, a graduate of West Point, was the pilot. His crew was made up of men from Pennsylvania, Kentucky, Ohio, California, New Jersey, Montana and Indiana. Matthew "Smitty" Smith sat next to Wickham as copilot. John Dorsey, the navigator, was responsible for getting the men to the target and bringing them back to their base. Daniel LaHurd was responsible for accurately dropping bombs onto targets. Gerald Fischer, the radio operator, was responsible for communications and manning the topside machine gun. Albert Greenway, the engineer, had the dual function as the go-to guy for any malfunctions with the plane and as the top turret gunner. Samuel Traser, Gerald Stillson, Sidney Beardshaw and Dell Oliver had the responsibility of defending their Flying Fortress with accurate shooting of their .50-caliber machine guns.

Each of these airmen had a different history, a different story. They had grown up playing different sports, working different jobs, studying different subjects and falling for different women. But these unique individuals over time would become one crew with only one job, one goal and one interest. The glue that bonded these men together was the single task of completing their missions and returning home alive.

LaHurd quickly developed camaraderie with his new crew members. The men flew practice missions day in and day out. They ate together. They slept in the same tents and barracks together. They slowly changed from separate individuals into a unit.

Daniel wrote home:

> *We flew yesterday afternoon and it was the navigators day to work. He had to calibrate all the instruments—after he finished that we flew over the gunnery range and fired all the workable guns on the plane. I really laid those .50-calibers in there with that nose gun. You wouldn't believe the noise they make, they shake the plane and boy do they smoke.*

Wickham, Smitty, Stegner and LaHurd spent most of their off time hanging around the officers' club drinking beers or sodas, talking about ladies and recent events in the war and going on short visits to the nearest town for entertainment. As LaHurd's associations with his crew matured, he also met an Irishman from the Bronx, a man who quickly became his best friend.

Daniel walked into the officers' club at Pyote and saw a poker game off in the corner. The club itself had been noticeably thrown up in a hurry. Windows were unlevel. Joints in the floor were uneven. On rainy days, the roof leaked. It didn't house much except a small bar, some tables, a couch, some cushioned chairs and two billiard tables accompanied by crooked cue sticks. Two ceiling fans hung from exposed cross beams overhead. But none of the officers complained. It was a place to relax, chat and have fun.

Four airmen sat with their cards, beers and cash spread in front of them. One officer was enjoying himself more than the others. His high-pitched laugh and thick Bronx accent resonated throughout the officers' club. The other three men at the table couldn't help but laugh along with the buoyant personality who appeared to be managing the game. Daniel walked over to the table with a beer in hand and threw down his cash. The men introduced themselves with handshakes.

The jovial New Yorker said, "Glad to meet you, Danny Boy. The name's Ryan, Arthur Ryan."

LaHurd settled in, and after an hour of cards, the game ended when Ryan's sure winning flush was beat by Danny Boy's full house.

With a red face, Ryan yelled, "You son-of-a-bitch!"

Danny began to chuckle, Ryan smirked and the two men began to laugh uncontrollably. Danny Boy stood up and walked to the bar, where he grabbed Ryan a beer. The conversation and jokes between the two bombardiers flowed like the drinks in their mugs. Ryan couldn't remember the last time he had laughed so hard, and Daniel couldn't recall the last time he had so much fun with someone after just cleaning out their wallet.

Arthur Ryan was a nice-looking man with a smile full of white teeth—a smile the ladies always seemed to notice. His optimism and wisecracks about the war calmed many of his fellow airmen's fears. He was constantly making jokes and had a knack for learning everyone's name. From a conservative Irish family, Ryan was respectful and polite as a result of his Catholic education but tough from his upbringing in the Bronx. He loved women, cigars, wine and poker. His accent, accompanied by wit and gallantry, attracted the ladies' attention. Put him in his military uniform, stick a cigarette in his mouth, let him start talking and he became irresistible to women. Ryan's hilariously unpredictable personality made for a perfect match with Danny Boy.

Daniel explained to his parents in a letter, "I met my new good buddy Ryan in a poker game last week. My full-house beat his flush, he called me a son of a bitch and we became pals! Kinda strange how friendships are built but this guy is a class act, real swell I tell you."

Mischievous, Ryan always seemed to talk his way out of any trouble that he and Danny Boy quite frequently seemed to conjure up. But aside from his hilarious personality and audacious behavior, he was also a family man. He was the only other officer whom Daniel came across who set aside a portion of the day to write home to his beloved mother.

LaHurd's number of daily letters was growing. He was now writing to his brother Calvin, his family in Akron and his girlfriend, Madeline. His correspondence to his sweetheart was long and filled with positive news. He wrote to her about his plans after the war. He filled his letters with charming lines and extravagant promises, his hopes and his dreams.

After spending only forty days at Pyote, Daniel and his new crew were off to Ephrata, Washington. Seven other crews accompanied the Wickham crew to the far northwestern state. Ryan's crew was part of the relocation squadron.

Nov. 6, 1943
Ephrata, Washington

Dear Folks

Well! we finally arrived here after a four day train ride. We left Pyote Monday at 7 P.M. and arrived here at 11 P.M. last nite. We had a nice train ride and went thru some beautiful country—really a nice trip. Ryan, Wickham and myself shared a stateroom on the train. It was much nicer traveling by troop train than if we had traveled by ourselves because we wouldn't have gotten Pullmans. We traveled by a round about way—Pyote to Ft Worth to Denver Colo.—Billings Mon.—Spokane and Ephrata. Played poker all the way up here and I believe I'm about $50 ahead—not bad considering my luck—which is far from good.

I don't know what the setup here is yet but when I do I'll let you know. The camp is run Piss Poor from what we hear but that won't bother me any. We have a nice barracks and a much nicer officers club than we had at Pyote. I don't believe we'll get much flying time here due to the weather. The weather here is nice and cool and I suspect it will get mighty cold here soon. Change in climate will do me good. The air is so much nicer here than in Texas.

Our enlisted men are going to get ten day leaves in a few days—that is if they haven't had one in the last six months. So I guess we'll go to ground school till they come back. Pity they didn't give them leaves at Pyote—now they have an extra 1000 miles or so to travel—most of them won't be able to make it home in that time.

Well I'll close now.

Love Dan

LaHurd's expectations were correct. The enlisted men went on furlough, visiting family across the country or chumming around in the nearest city. Since the enlisted men made up the majority of the crew, the planes never left the ground for the first two weeks. Even if the entire crew had been present, the thick fogs and misty, overcast days would have forestalled any attempt at a practice mission. Daniel and the other officers spent their time in ground school, at the officers' club and on occasions partook in some outdoor activities.

"I went hunting with Wickham yesterday. We stopped at Tech Supply and got ourselves a couple of automatic shotguns and some shells and out we went to the wild of the northwest. The pilot got two ducks—and all I got was wet and tired feet," Daniel wrote home.

Nov. 24, 1943
Ephrata, Washington

Dear Folks.

I received the goodies O.K.—so thanks loads—Mel's mother also sent me some ButtLawee and Mel sent me a box of candy so I'm well supplied for sometime. I also received the Tshirts—so I must thank you once again. Your all so swell—it really pays to have such swell folks.

They've kept us pretty busy going to ground school everyday this week. The weather is still bad around here for flying so we've been going to school instead. The Group is leaving here for Utah this coming week as the pilots have to get some flying time in as the Group is due for overseas duty by the 1ˢᵗ of the year. Boy!! what a Pi-- Poor Group this is. I really feel sory for the poor suckers that are stuck with this outfit. I just can't express myself in telling you how lousy it is and how poor it's run. Worst I've run into since being in the army.

GOOD NEWS

I guess you know I have a West Point Pilot—well! they made a mistake when they sent us from Pyote to here—there are four W.P. pilots and we're—I mean pilots and crews are leaving this Friday for Rapid City S. Dak. and maybe we'll only be there a short time and than leave for Florida—I heard a rumor today that the bombardiers from Hondo are up for 1ˢᵗ Lt. but they have to wait till their pilots get theirs first—Just a rumor.

I guess you misunderstood me about the Beacon. *I receive one from Hondo and Pyote yet and those are the ones I want canceled. I'll send you my new address as soon as I find it out. I'm really feeling swell now that I'm leaving this Group.*

Love Dan

The West Point pilots and their crews were off to Rapid City, South Dakota. In Rapid City, the four West Point–led crews were officially assigned to the 483ʳᵈ Bombardment Group. The men transplanted from Ephrata only stayed for a week in Rapid City before moving out to MacDill Air Base in Tampa, Florida. Fortunately, Ryan had a West Point pilot as well and traveled with Danny Boy.

By the second week of December 1943, the 483ʳᵈ Bombardment Group was gathering in Tampa. While at MacDill, Wickham's crew lost their navigator to another crew, and Traser, one of their gunners, was transferred to a refueling position within the AAF. Robert Stegner became the new navigator, and John Huntley took over the vacant gunner position.

Daniel wrote home to his father, "MacDill Air Base is the most well organized military facility in the country. Haven't seen anything like this yet since I left for Santa Ana. We've changed up some of our crewmembers this week. Sad to see those fellows go."

Monday December
Tampa, Florida

Dear Folks

With a pipe in my mouth and a long day over—I sit here thinking what to write—so I'll first start off by thanking you for that twenty dollar Xmas gift—Boy! I wonder what your thinking after receiving my telegram— nothing small about me—figured Mel being here and maybe a three day pass—Friday thru Sunday—might get home—if not I can show Mel a goodtime—Playboy LaHurd—with Pop's money—feel like a heel—but take the money from my account—one of these days I'll catch up on myself and will be able to repay it to D.E. LaHurd + Co.

Show what kind of a schedule I went thru today—up at 4:30— down to operations by 5:00 A.M.—briefing at 6:00—takeoff at

7:00 landed at 12:30—eat from 12:30 to 1:15—1:15 to 2:00 athletics—2:30 to 5:30 school rough isn't it—like that everyday we fly and if we don't fly we sit around operations for five hours doing nothing but getting Pissed OFF and than off to school for the rest of the day.

They have a curfew around here off the streets by 11:30 P.M. and they mean it—fine if your caught—fine ya for everything around here—not saluting $75—rough isn't it and 2ⁿᵈ Lt's salute 2ⁿᵈ Lt's and they do it and like it. Trouble is III Bomber Command Headquarters is located here at MacDill and there is plenty of rank here—poor 2ⁿᵈ Looies—have a couple of star Generals on the field here—rough isn't it.

Pronto Must Do

Give the Beacon *my correct address from Sq. to serial number (0741271) I receive a paper about once a week due to that—sure are rough about the correct address around here—still haven't received any mail from Ephrata or Rapid City probably due to Xmas rush.*

Oh! take me back to Pyote.

We are going to a flight commanders school—that is the pilots are—and after finishing here—we'll get some more crews in to fill out the group than we'll start our phase training over again.

This training is getting to be a bore or a rut—We almost completed our three phases than the West Point crews were pulled out to come here. The Group we left at Ephrata are about thru with their training now—about two or three more weeks they should be on their way over the deep blue pond. We'll probably leave Tampa for someplace in Georgia in a few weeks—rumor you know—I guess you know by this time not to believe the rumors I write—to start our first phase training—hope so anyway—sure would like to get away from most of the rank around here and go to a place where one can stay out after 11:30 P.M. Bet that makes you happy.

Tomorrow we're on a different schedule—ground school in the morning and fly in the afternoon—and our crew is scheduled to fly tomorrow—we only have three planes in our Sq. now and we have six crews and its seems like our crew gets most of the flying—I should kick, I've only flew once since being here and twice at Ephrata—about three flights in two months time—sure am cheating the government.

I'm still sweating out a letter from Cal—should receive one soon, now that he is back at the ole homestead.

Did I tell ya that I received Lous + Als gift—if not—thanks.

Tell Lou to take a peek at the dress I bought Mel—really wicked—best they had for $49.95—don't tell me Lou that that is too much—I spent the only day I've had off looking for a gift—really had to rack my little brain so finally the blue wick dress caught my eye—you know blue to match her eyes—or is it green eyes SHIT. Bet she doesn't wear it as is.

Well! I best close for now—so good nite and pleasant dreams—I know I will—cause Mel is on her way.

Feeling swell—maybe getting up early does it.

Love

Dan

After months of training, the crew was virtually ready for combat. Each man now knew his job in detail as a result of the countless hours of practice over the past few months. Each bomber had its place in a squadron. LaHurd was part of the 817th Squadron. Each of the four squadrons made up the 483rd Bombardment Group. The pilots grew comfortable flying in formation as their practice missions littered the sky with precisely situated Fortresses. The time to head to Europe, where the fight was raging, had finally drawn near. LaHurd began to make appropriate arrangements as rumors of deployment overseas floated through MacDill. Battle was no longer months or years away but potentially weeks. Daniel would finally become an aerial warrior who would soon be called upon to help defeat Hitler. As 1944 neared, so, too, did Daniel's chances of going to war.

He was promoted to first lieutenant, strengthening his confidence. Traveling overseas was now a reality. The need for bomber crews grew as missions were being run day and night over enemy Europe.

He sent a letter home to his girlfriend. Inside the envelope was a train ticket and a letter pleading that Madeline make the trip down to Tampa. He needed to see her before being shipped overseas. Madeline beat her return letter to the Sunshine State. Daniel's final days in the United States were spent with her, staying in a nearby hotel. While he was off at the base for the majority of the day, she wandered over to the officers' club, where she spent her days chatting with girlfriends and wives of other officers. While there, the women sat and mentally prepared themselves for what they predicted was going to be many long days of war and worry. In the evenings, Daniel and Madeline spent every minute together.

She wrote home to Joseph and Mary:

Danny and I have been able to see each other every day since I've been here. I have been taking a bus and going out to camp to visit him in the evenings as they have a very nice officer's club and nicer theater we can go to. I have also met all of his buddies who are very nice. I met his buddy Ryan and they get along just like brothers.

The hardest letter Daniel had to write home was the letter that made arrangements for his possible death. The difficulty didn't come from his fear of dying but from the fear of knowing that the topic was going to upset his family.

Wed. December Noon
Tampa, Florida

Dear Folks and how are ye all—fine I'm hoping. Well! Mel arrived safe, sound and much tired but after a good nites sleep she once more looks and acts beautiful.

I believe we'll get married Sat. evening and on the double at that as I won't be able to get a three day pass and I'll have to be back early Sunday morning to fly but I'll be off from Sunday noon till early Monday morning for school—no event is big enough in the army to allow officers three day passes.

Well! Folks the time is getting short before I go over to help pin Hitler's ears back and in case something does happen to me—cause I hear they use real live bullets over there—here's how I want my personnel affairs taken care of.

The $1000 insurance and the money in our bank account will stay in the LaHurd clan—I mean Mike, Fred and Cal can help start a business with that and what they have—next the $10,000 government insurance—money that Mel and I will be able to save—if I have any money in the Fort San Houston Bank in San Antonio, Texas—will all go to Mel. She'll be well taken care of if anything should happen to me she will also receive six months salary which will amount to over $1300 or $1400.

I'll send you the proper forms as I've made you my Power of Attorney and you will be able to sign for all government checks due to me.

Well! that takes care of that for the time being. I've told Mel my plans and she also agrees with me whole heartidly about everything.

I'm feeling swell except for a little nose cold—how could it be little with my big nose.

Love
Dan

Left: Arthur Ryan.

Middle: Arthur Ryan stands at the far right atop a B-17 Flying Fortress, nicknamed "Fort Alamo II."

Bottom: *Top row, left to right*: Wickham (pilot), Smith (copilot), Stegner (navigator), LaHurd (bombardier). *Bottom row, left to right*: Oliver (engineer), Stillson (right waist gunner), Beardshaw (ball turret gunner), Greenway (left waist gunner), Fischer (radio), Huntley (tail gunner).

With the imminent danger of combat immediately looming, Daniel asked Madeline to be his wife. She accepted. Their wedding was small, but neither of them would have changed it for the world. Her hair was perfect. The Catholic church was situated only a few miles from the sandy beaches of Tampa, Florida, just outside MacDill, its peaked roof sheltering them from the southern heat. Open doors allowed a soft breeze to flow inside, pushing the pungent smells of incense and candle smoke around the room. Daniel and Ryan, his best man, were perfectly dressed in their military jackets, slacks, chocolate brown shirts and khaki neckties. Ryan stood at Daniel's side, keeping the groom's jitters to a minimum with his wisecracks. Madeline looked more beautiful than ever. She made her way down the aisle in a new dress given to her as a gift the day before by Arthur Ryan. She carried a small bouquet of yellow daisies. Her smile beamed brighter than the Florida sun. Ryan proudly patted his best friend's shoulder as the bride stood face to face with her husband-to-be. Madeline Ezzie became Madeline LaHurd on February 5, 1943.

In part, Daniel had been lucky. He had been fortunate enough to spend a month with his new bride. Many soldiers across the country married and immediately departed for battle. A number of those men never returned home to see their wives again. Soldiers often deployed for Europe or the Pacific to later learn their wives were pregnant. Some of those new dads never returned home to see their babies.

For the brief time remaining to them, Daniel and Madeline were happy together. He kept busy with his training, and she watched the minutes of the day tick away until Daniel was free to visit. The days went quickly. They both knew that deployment was close. Madeline frequented the church they were married in. Often, she knelt before the altar, tears streaming down her cheeks, and asked God to be with her husband and return him safely to her arms. These days became more and more emotionally wrenching. The last letter sent from Florida to Akron was short. Because Daniel was so busy with training, his wife wrote to the LaHurds:

Tuesday Feb. 15, 1944
Tampa, Florida

Dear Folks
Here's hoping everyone at home is fine and as happy as we are.
Right now Dan is on a very long schedule, working quite a few hours. Some days they have been flying mornings and others afternoon. Tomorrow there is supposed to be a formation of about 500 or 600 planes and as

Danny flies afternoon he will be in it. You see General "Hap" Arnold and quite a few other high ranking officers are visiting at MacDill.

Yesterday we were going to write and suggest that you and Mom come down here to visit Dan. Only rumors have it, that they will be confined to the post after Friday Feb. 18 until sent to a staging area. Then he would like to have you visit him then, as he wants to see you before going overseas. I'm hoping and praying this is one rumor that isn't so. Only we shall let you know definitely.

We are still staying in the hotel as everything is so uncertain and them not knowing how long they will be here. Only if they are confined after this week. I will go home and if not, we will get another place to stay.

Otherwise, we are very happy and getting along fine.

Love,
Dan and Mel

Daniel's deployment orders came. He was off to Europe. Madeline made her way back to Akron by train. By March 1944, bombers were flying missions over Europe every day and every night. Their targets differed, but the death-defying odds never did. All Daniel wanted to do was get over there, help end the war and get back home to his wife.

Chapter 9

OVER THE DEEP BLUE POND

March 6, 1944–July 17, 1944

From now on we shall bomb Germany on an ever-increasing scale, month by month, year by year, until the Nazi regime has either been exterminated by us or—better still—torn to pieces by the German people themselves.
—*Prime Minister Winston Churchill*

Daniel leaned back against the confusion of interwoven bark of an aged olive tree. The twisted roots crawled across the ground and disappeared deep into the Italian soil and limestone on the foothills of the province of Foggia, Italy, on July 17, 1944. Beyond the trees, the landscape slowly leveled off into a flat coastal plain, giving way to the beaches of the Adriatic Sea. Disturbed by occasional coastal breezes, olives fell intermittently around the tree's base. Surrounded by this peaceful vista, Daniel recalled his route here. A group of 646 crew members of the 483rd Bombardment Group received their orders for departure from the United States to the Italian peninsula and the province of Foggia in late February. The Fifteenth Air Force, commanded by General Nathan Twining, had chosen Bari, Foggia, as its headquarters months earlier. The strategically placed bases in Italy allowed the newly formed Fifteenth to strike targets in southern Europe, targets out of the range of the Eighth Air Force based throughout southern England. The Eighth was delivering devastating blows to Germany's infrastructures, causing the Nazis to move many of their factories south. This put the enemy in perfect position for the newly established air force in Italy. Germany was surrounded with the possibility of attacks from both England in the north and Italy in the south.

The group's journey overseas was a lengthy one, nearly one month. Because the large fortified B-17s lacked the range to travel from the coast of the United States to the Allied nations of Europe, the 483rd had to hop down the eastern coast of the United States to South America and to the northern regions of Africa until landing at designated bases in Europe.

Wickham's crew first traveled by rail from Tampa to Hunter Field in Savannah, Georgia, where they were issued combat clothing and equipment and assigned a B-17 for the flight overseas. The journey started on March 6 when the crews left the port of embarkation at Morrison Field, West Palm Beach, Florida. From Florida, the crews traveled to Trinidad, then to Natal, Brazil. From there, they were at their closest point to the paralleling beaches of Africa separated by the Atlantic Ocean. The lackluster flight from Brazil to Dakar, West Africa, was smooth though lengthy, making Daniel respect the size of the expansive body of salt water below. From Dakar, the 483rd traveled to Morocco, then to Djedeida, Tunisia, and finally to Torotella, Italy. Here they stayed for two weeks awaiting the construction of their new base at Sterparone.

LaHurd's first letter home in over a month was sent from his temporary base:

> *April 1, 1944*
> *Italy*
>
> *Dear Folks*
> *Well I'm still knocking around the world and right now I'll probably be in Italy for the duration—if lucky. We left Africa several days ago and are now somewhere in Italy. It's not bad country—rolling lands and mountains in the not too for distance—really nice—nothing like home though. The weather is fairly cold during early morning and evening but during the day it's fairly warm. Today we had a strong wind blowing and took part of the officers club's roof off—kinda made it pretty cool out today.*
>
> *I haven't flown and the way things look I probably won't for several days. This isn't our own field—we're just assigned here till our field is completed—wish it were though as they've been here for sometime and are well established. They sure have a beautiful officers club—something we won't have at our field—lucky if we have any at all.*
>
> *I'm still living in tents and like it but I'm thru with mess kits as long as I'm at this field—imagine eating at tables again and have waiters too.*

Went to town today and had me a wonderful shower—sure felt good. Couple of cents and we got warm shower. We got clothes washed by some locals. Sure feel bad for some of those locals. Speak of rough times. Well! I'm still feeling better than swell and am fine—so don't worry.

Love

Dan

Torotella, Italy, was the home base of the 99th Bombardment Group. Here, during their two-week tenure, novice crews of the 483rd were given the opportunity to fly with veterans for some real combat experience. Fred Wickham quickly jumped at the chance. He piloted a B-17 to Sofia, Bulgaria, on March 30, just after he and his crew had arrived in Italy.

LaHurd and Smitty anxiously awaited Wickham's return from the mission. They had a number of burning questions for their buddy. The flak—was it really as bad as the others had made it out to be? Did the sky literally turn black from exploding shells? Was the shrapnel truly unavoidable? How did those *Luftwaffe* planes maneuver?

While the B-17s from the Sofia mission made their final approach for the runway, LaHurd and Smitty scurried outside from the officers' club to meet and greet their now experienced pilot. LaHurd held a cigar in his hand, ready to congratulate Wickham. Daniel and Smitty watched as bomber after bomber touched down. The two men counted off each plane as it landed.

Wickham's B-17 never returned.

Flying with a crew from the 2nd Bombardment Group, disaster had struck for Wickham when another Fortress was caught in prop-wash and flipped and crashed onto Wickham's aircraft. At twenty thousand feet, the incident had been catastrophic. Both planes had crumbled in midair. Wickham, along with the other crew members inside both planes, had perished.

Soon after the charcoaled debris of the crash trickled to the ground, letters from the AAF would arrive at the homes of Walter Crowl in Wilmington, Delaware; Erwin Rubinstein in Brooklyn, New York; Orville W. Reilly in Cincinnati, Ohio; Richard Luksch in Buffalo, New York; Homer Mckee in Wenatchee, Washington; Andrew Wargn in Newark, New Jersey; William Marion in Columbia, South Carolina; Pator O'Grady in Milford, Connecticut; Tony Morriah in Jennings, Louisiana; and Fred Wickham in Baltimore, Maryland, informing their fathers, mothers and wives that their sons and husbands had honorably been killed in action.

Daniel's pilot, a good friend, was gone, dead, killed in action. Suddenly for the Akronite, the war became very real. The dangers became personal. Wickham had become the first fatality of the 483rd.

Daniel wrote home:

> *Wickham—ya wanted to know what happened to him. Well! one bright night he told us that we (the crew) were going to fly a mission with him the next morning—come the next morning—we all went to briefing got the dope on the mission and were ready to go down the flight line—when Wickham came up to me and said "Sorry but I have to fly with another crew today—maybe we can fly together tomorrow"—well! he and the crew he flew with that day never came back. Fate was with us that day...*

LaHurd's years of practice and rigorous training were finally going to be put to the test. The days of hearing stories and reading reports about air battles were behind him. It was time for the real thing.

Lieutenant Jack Kent from Molalla, Oregon, replaced Wickham as the crew's pilot. LaHurd, Smitty, Stegner, Greenaway, Fischer, Beardshaw, Huntley, Stillson and Oliver were going to travel over enemy territory and confront the Nazis from miles above the ground. The planned mission was thought to be a milk run. The cement works at Split, Yugoslavia, was supposed to be a quick flight north. Few problems were forecasted, and enemy engagement was predicted to be light.

The expected humdrum mission quickly turned treacherous as Kent and his crew crossed the Yugoslavian border. As blankets of black shrapnel began to fill the sky, each airman's survival became a matter of chance. It was worse than any inexperienced airman could have imagined or any veteran wanted to recall. There was absolutely no defense against the flak.

Deafening explosions echoed through the open sky. Shockwaves smashed at the aircrafts' thin bodies. Suddenly the Preston crew, flying off LaHurd's left side, was obliterated by the murderous black clouds. The bomber's wing folded, and shrapnel sliced through the aircraft like a warm knife through butter. Within seconds, Preston's B-17 turned to fragments.

The group completed their terrifying mission in just over four hours. It was the single scariest incident of LaHurd's life. To think he was going to have to do this over and over again. He winced at the thought and prayed for his lost comrades.

The very next day, Daniel traveled over enemy territory again, this time on a five-hour mission to bomb a railroad-marshaling yard in Yugoslavia. It was equally as hair-raising as his first. Because of censorship, Daniel's letters home couldn't do justice to the actual emotions involved in the intense flights over enemy territory, but he kept on writing no matter the circumstances.

April 15, 1944
Italy

Dear Folks

Well! what do ya know I finally received a letter from ya today—dated March 10—and was more than mighty happy to receive it. Sure was a long time since I heard from ya last—come to think of it—I saw ya last. I also received a letter from Cal and was glad he is staying in dear ole U.S.A.— this is no place for a lover like Cal.

I'm still living the life—wasn't scheduled to fly today so I didn't get up till 12:00—seems I've got my civilian habit back again—sleeping late as I please—would have slept later but Ryan woke me up. Good ole Ryan finally got here a few days ago, after nearly a month ride on the boat.

Mighty glad to hear Cal's bank account is growing—maybe he, Mike, Fred and I can go into business. Me, I'm going to try and send Mel at least $200 every month but for sure she'll get a $100 and a $25 bond every month—I have that much in allotments to her. I've sent her $400 so far this month—which isn't bad—Oh! happy cards—I guess I'm about $500 ahead so far this month.

It seems that I have a couple of combat missions in.

Well! that's all for now except that I'm feeling O.K.—so you all best take care of yourself and be happy. Is everybody happy. I'd be a helluva lot happier if I was home.

Love
Dan

———

April 20, 1944
Italy

Dear Folks

Yip!! It's me—tired but feeling swell. Tired from flying today—I still have three combat missions to my credit—should have four but twice we went all the way into enemy territory but couldn't see the target for the overcast. We fly an average of two days and rest one—that is if the weather is good.

Well! my luck is still holding out in cards—I guess I've cleared around $800 or $900 this month so far—I guess Mel is the big gainer as I've sent her $700 so far this month—not bad ah pop. Who knows maybe I'll have enough to go in business if my luck keeps up.

We're suppose to move to our own field come this Sunday.

Pa, you keep asking me if I want anything just ask for it—well! I'm taking ya up on it—I know you expected me to ask for candy well! your wrong—ya know what I'd really like is some can baked beans (Heinz preferably)—chicken soup and spagehette—sure would be swell if you could send me a few cans every week and change the menu every once in awhile. Sure could stand some R-B cookies too.

Ya know it sure is hard to write a letter when ya have to be careful of what ya say—and I always was short on words anyhow.

We have a softball team in our Sq. and Daniel is their star short stop— We played an Anti Aircraft outfit the other nite and beat them 7 to 1. I started the game off by hitting a homer the first time at bat and put our team in the lead 1 to 0. Got 3 out of 4 which isn't bad.

Well!! that's about all for now except I'm feeling O.K. and hope you all are too.

Got another letter from Cal—which makes two—one from Mike—one from Boo Boo—one from Lou—one from you all and basket full from Mel.

Love Dan

After bombing a marshaling yard in northern Italy, the next day, April 21, the group destroyed an aircraft factory in Belgrade, Yugoslavia. With only one day of rest, LaHurd and the group bombarded an Me 109 fighter factory in the suburbs of Vienna, Austria. The following day, the crew revisited Belgrade, knocking out another railroad marshaling yard.

By the end of April, the 483rd had moved from Torotella to their newly erected home base, Sterparone Airfield. It was dank and tough living at first. Sterparone was without barracks; the men lived in tents. An officers' club was imaginary. Open latrines and mess kits were the way of life there. For the first few months, even showers were nonexistent. And the airmen constantly battled the oversized Italian mosquitoes.

Daniel's missions through hostile skies took an immediate toll on his mental state. He waged daily battle with a variety of conflicting emotions— exhaustion and fear, jubilation at completed missions, a sense of pride and honor, appreciation of his luck, confusion and anger at the untimely death of his comrades. No classroom, textbook or training mission could have ever prepared him for the terrors and stresses of active combat. The sounds, smells and sights could never be simulated. But even under these terrible circumstances, LaHurd took pains to portray his combat experiences as ordinary in his letters home:

> *May 3, 1944*
> *Italy*

Dear Folks

I'm fine and really doing O.K. and I'm not lying a bit when I say I kinda enjoy it a little bit—except when I get the hell scared outa me and that only happened a couple of times. Couple too many though.

I haven't flown since Sunday but we did take off yesterday and get half way to our target and had to turn back—bad weather—I guess that makes me nine raids and five dry runs—only sad part about it, dry runs don't count.

We got paid last nite and after having insurance, allottements, mess and a $25 bond taken out of my pay, I still received $152 which isn't bad. Seeing it was payday, the LaHurd Klub opened up last nite after being closed for three days—(reason no money around) and my luck was still fairly good. I ended up about $100 winners but after everyone paid me back what they owed me I had a little bit over $500. So too much cash isn't good for my pockets—burns holes in them—so I went to town today and like a good husband and a good uncle I had some money orders made out $300 for Mel and $50 for Neil. I promised myself I'd send Neil $50 to buy a bike with and me being a man of my word—especially to myself, I did—so now I'm happy—Neil is happy—Beulah worried, Ma's worried and your worried. Neil will hurt himself but you're only young once. Ah! I can remember the day when I was young and Ma said "I'll buy you a bike if you pass reading this year"—seems I never could pass.

While in town today Ryan, I and a few other fellows went and had ourselves a beautiful shower and after that—well!! we put on the feed bag and I mean feed bag. We each had from 3 to 4 helpings and a gallon of wine. Really made hogs of ourselves. Ah! they must of known I was going to pay the bill. Cost me $22.00 but all good gambling clubs buy there best customers meals—anyway I hope to win that and a lot more back tonite.

Mel writes and tells me you haven't been receiving many letters from me. I don't want you to think I haven't been writing you because I have. So far I think I've only received around four letter from you and I know you're writing ten times that many. Today I received an Easter card from you and it was dated *April 7 I* also have received your letters of *March 8 and mail of April 15,* the reason I think your letters take so long in getting here is because of the envelope—with Grocer's Institute on it—they probably think it's a business letter and don't give a damn when it gets here—so please try a change of envelopes.

Well! that's all for now—so bye for now and I hope this letter finds you all happy and feeling fine. I know you're not too happy now but you soon will be when all us LaHurd boys get back and give with a big hug and kiss—so these kisses *XXXX* will have to do till I can deliver them by Danny Boy.

Love
Dan

—⁓—

May 9, 1944
Italy

Dear Folks

I started to write this letter this morning but as far as I got was the date—Ryan came in and wanted me to go in town with him and eat—that got me—eat—so I went. We had our usually three helpings and a bottle of wine and than returned to camp. We also went to town yesterday—had a shower—ate—bought ten bunches of green onions and *80 eggs.* Them eggs sure taste good, fried in butter with plenty of onions mixed in. Had about four last nite before going to bed and three this morning. Gave a few of the young boys in town some loose change. Boy how I feel for them. Just kids ya know. Poor as a stray dog.

Didn't fly yesterday or today either but we flew three mission before that—which makes a total of *12* for me. The last mission sure was a tough one though.

I've been to Foggia several times to buy my rations and to get coffee and donuts at Red Cross, but all you can do in town except maybe take in a movie but I've seen most of the pictures back in the States.

Mighty glad to hear Fred and his honey are making with the knot come *June 10ᵗʰ.* Lucky guy at least he'll be able to spend more time with his honey than I did.

How's Mike—is he in yet?

What's new about Cal.?

I still haven't received much mail from you so far—can count them on my one hand—I know it isn't your fault but I'm sure they'll all catch up with me soon.

Ya know it's mighty hard to write a letter here, especially when ya haven't a letter to refer to and ya have to be careful of what ya say.

I'm feeling swell and eating more than my share but I'd trade all the food here for a good dish of kibbeh.

Well! I best close now—so bye for now and please don't worry. P.S. my poker luck is still good.

Love

Dan

—∿∿—

May 21, 1944

Italy

Dear Folks

Well! dear people I sure hope you're all fine and happy—as for me I couldn't feel any better even if I used my hands. I just finished writing to Mel and Cal and last but not least by a long shot you. Ya know if I try real hard today I might get caught up on my letter writing—what makes me hate to write letters? Must take after Ma—I can only remember one letter she ever wrote and I can probably say—that was to me. I still think I have it somewhere in my papers—not sure though.

So Fred is getting all set for the big day—can't believe Fred is getting married—couldn't believe it either when I made with a ball and chain.

I'm glad to hear the food is on the way that I asked for but please don't send any more Spam or potted meats—Army lives on Spam. I give my spam to the locals and sometimes get some of the best noodles in the world.

Gosh!! I sure would like to see the house now—I hear it really is the berries—hear Ma is saving the new chair for Cal and I to fight over—that isn't fair—Cal is helleva lot bigger than I am and he no doubt would beat the living day lights outta me—Guess you'll have to get another as I sure don't want to tangle with Cal—no how (I had to quit here—as it was time to eat dinner) (also played a little ball).

Well! I guess ya all know by now that I'm about the loafings person in Italy—no kidding I've only been on five raids so far this month and the other 16 days I've loafed or gone to San Severo. I only flew once this last week—scheduled for a practice mission though but it never came off—due to weather—funny thing I asked to be put on the loading list for it to—shows I'm really eager—and that's the first time I ever asked for extra practice and no-doubt my last time.

Yesterday Ryan and I went to Foggia and I bought my weekly rations of gum, candy and cigarettes and had ice cream and lemonade at the Red Cross and than came back to camp. Big Day.

I guess you're wondering if all the crew are still intact—they sure are and I guess they're just as eager as I am to fly every mission so we can get our 50 in and beat it back home for 30 days or longer.

I'm glad to hear Mike is still home and hope to Christ he stays there. Tell Beulah I received her swell letter and tell her to not let the kids get her down any lower than flak gets us guys—probably have to send her to a rest camp—anyhow that's what they do to us—send us to a rest camp after we complete so many missions that is if we need it and right now I sure don't as I've had plenty of rest just loafing. Also, tell Lou I've been receiving her letters and if I must say so, I really enjoy them—she sure puts in all the dope—about every dope and things—tell Mike his letters are really pilling up on me and I'm having a helleva time reading them all—just like mine are on him.

How are the kids? Did Neil receive his money for his bike yet? Make sure he passes in school before you get it for him.

How is everyone? fine I hope—me I'm still healthy—poor—and dumb—so I say—but Ma knows different—don't ya Ma. That's it stick up for me. Hey!! Ma did ya get the flowers I sent ya for Mother's day—I was too late to send ya some for Easter—Easter—it past + I didn't know—seems I flew a raid Easter—helluva time to kill people don't ya think—seems we don't think—they think for us. Just so we're all happy—what's the difference—right? right. Ya are happy aren't ya?

Well! I best close now and hope this letter finds you all swell

Love
Dan

P.S. Say hello to everyone for me.
P.S. Please send me some goodies—thanks.

—~~~—

May 28, 1944
Italy

Dear Folks
Here it is Sunday and a day of rest even way over here. I've been taking it easy all day and right now I'm heating water—yip!! it's about time I shaved and it being Sunday—I thought it'd be a good day to make off with my four day ole beard.

The Beacon *finally caught up with me—all forty of them and I've been spending the last three days reading them. It sure is swell to read the home town paper and find out how the war is making out.*

I've only flown three times in the past week—which makes me a total of 17 missions—We really had two long hops this last week—longest ever flown from this theater. Too long to suit me.

The last day off Smitty and I hitched a ride in a plane and went near the front lines to a British field—only about 20 minutes by air and landed there. While sitting around someone suggested a little game of poker—so we jumped in the plane and played a four handed game in the waist—well in about 20 minutes the game broke up and I had won around $95—all in the last pot—so Smitty suggested we buy a motorcycle off one of the Limeys (British)—so Smitty bought one for $25 and I paid $50—seeing as I was never on one before—well the first time I let out the clutch it almost threw me but ya know me "Ride em LaHurd"—well after a little practice—I thought I was good enough to ride it the 65 miles back to camp—so Smitty and I started back around 3 P.M.—five miles from where we bought them Smitty's bike broke down and after trying for three hours to start it—we had no luck—not even the Limeys who stopped to help us had any luck—and their own make to. Well! seeing as it was getting late and I had no lights and we sure had to get back for briefing—well! we left it lay on the road— hoping someone would run over the darn thing with a truck and Smitty hopped on the back end of mine—well we rode over more mountains and roads that we call ditches back home and only traveled about 25 miles— Boy!! those roads—I wouldn't go over them again for love nor money—no wonder the battle for Italy is taking so long—Now I know.

While on the road we met a Major from our outfit riding a jeep and seeing it was dark and we had no lights he picked us up—bike and all— otherwise we would never had made it back in time for briefing—My TZ [ass] is still sore.

Well that's all for now—Ryan just came in—and we're off to chow.

Feeling swell
Loads of Love
Dan

From the time the 483ʳᵈ had arrived at Sterparone, they were racking up missions all across southern Europe. Ploesti, Piatra, Sarayavo, Nis, Milan, Ferentino, Vienna, Wiener Neustadt, Budapest, Bucharest and Belgrade were among the 215 combat missions the group participated in throughout the war. LaHurd was dropping bombs on marshaling yards from Budapest to Milan. He was targeting aircraft factories and repair facilities, cement works, steel mills, tank works, harbors, communication networks, supply dumps and airfields.

By June, Air Force Command had altered strategies. Missions switched from bombing transportation routes and manufacturing facilities to bombing oil refineries and synthetic oil plants. The Allies' goal: bleed Germany dry of its fuel.

July 3, 1944
Italy

Dear Folks

Oh! Boy—I received letters today—six big letters—three from my honey—two from you and one from Lou. Lou's letters are always good—I get all the poop—gossip—news—advise on romance—and everything in general. I guess she best write more often. Hey! Lou how are the kids? fine I hope—How big is Allan getting to be and has he still got that LaHurd blond hair?—that is the question—and how is the toughie Mary Lou?—still fighting Linda Lou and whose doing the winning? Neil and his bike—how are they—I wonder if he is still losing his teeth—that is—as fast as I'm losing my fillings. Ma—how's she and the house—still buying furniture—hope she isn't worrying too much. Pa—how the hell are you—few more missions and I'll have more gray hairs than you. Mike and the fish—wonder who the biggest one is—still I'm going on one of those famous Mike fishing trips—still remember the swell times we had in Michigan and Canada—Oh! to have the quart of Canadian Club we broke in Canada. Al and the store—wonder if the bill collectors are getting paid any better. Beulah and her wild tribe—wonder if Neil has finally admitted she's boss. Lou and her house—who's taking down the wallpaper and sanding the floors—not me.

Ah! yes—me—how am I and what am I doing? I'm fine—I'd tell ya that anyway even if I wasn't but I am same as ya tell me—so there we're even. Missions—little rough, that is, some of them—others are milk runs (easy) but now I'm starting to go downhill—have 24 to go and those will be the ones I'll really sweat out. I've been fairly busy this week—what do I mean this week—happen to dawn on me—here it is only Monday—anyhow—I flew day before yesterday—yesterday—today [Piatra] and I'm flying again tomorrow. I wonder where the target will be—hope it's an easy one. We been changing our missions up a bit, and Boy are the new targets heavily defended. Can scare the shitskies out of ya. Remember those oil girls in Texas I used to like well we don't want those Nazis to have any of that black gold.

Ah! yes—mustn't forget to tell you about my poker playing this month. Well! payday I started off with a bang—lost $130—next day won $270—yesterday lost $130—if I could only get over the hump and lose $131—should be my turn to win tonite—but instead I thought I best write some letters. I wonder!—I wonder!! how I'd made out today if I'd have played—guess I'll never know.

Just as I started to write the letter—Ryan cooked some chili—tuna sandwiches with onions on raisin bread and water to wash it down—mighty tasty meal—and more than mighty good—had ample helpers tonite—seemed like everybody in the area got wind of it and all came to join the meal and did. That's the way it is in the army—when one guy gets something from home all his friends join in—one big unhappy family. Oh! yes yes—I received three cans of corn today—thanks again + again—Boy! that'll sure be good cooked in butter and that's the way I mean to cook it.

I've been receiving mail from Cal regularly—so I knew he wasn't in the invasion—really glad to hear that—be long time before Cal will get in it—seems they're using seasoned troops and I don't blame them. The mail was held up by the invasion as you probably already know.

Well! folks be good and I'll be good—fair enough. So with these words I close this letter—"Some letter huh!"

Love
Dan
XXXXXXXXXXX

P.S. I'd write more but we're having an early briefing tomorrow and it's now 10:35. Need my beauty rest—ya know. Say hello to everyone for me. I'd call this a real family letter. Gosh! I can't quit but I will—so the end.

His father had written to him, "Tomorrow is July 4th and I can't help but think back just a few years ago when I would take my boys to buy fireworks and here this fourth you and Cal are taking part in the greatest shooting exhibition the world has ever seen. Sometimes it all seems like a bad dream that will soon go away on awakening." On Independence Day, LaHurd's squadron destroyed an oil refinery in Romania. The mission was his longest to date, nearly seven and a half hours. More significantly, the heavily defended oil refinery was his twenty-fifth successfully completed mission. He was halfway to number fifty and home. "Ryan and I will kill a pint of C.C. that he has been saving. Big Doings—It won't be long and I'll be starting to go downhill now—25 to go Yipee," he victoriously wrote home to his parents.

His reward from the AAF for the amassed missions was rest camp. Veteran airmen were entitled to ten days off duty of relaxation and recreation. Rome, the Isle of Capri and Naples were the three main destinations for the Allied soldiers. There, the deserving combat veterans were treated like royalty.

July 15, 1944
Italy

Dear Folks

Safe and sound Dan reporting again from his little tent in the heart of Italy. All's well here—how about there?—everything O.K.—and how is everyone feeling?—that's good.

I got back from rest camp last nite around 10:00 P.M.—and what a ride that is from Naples to here—never saw so many mountain roads and curves—not since the last time I want to Naples—to top it off our truck broke down so all (30 of us) and baggage had to ride in one truck—little crowded. Smitty and I left Capri Tuesday and stayed the rest of our rest period in Naples. I hear Capri has some beautiful sights but I wouldn't know—never left the sack long enough to find out. One thing for sure the food was swell—ya know ya soon get tired of steaks and chicken. Everything was served to ya from silver plates—waiters with white coats—low ties—strictly high class stuff. Tell ma to polish the silver ware—they spoiled me here.

I received about three letters from ya yesterday plus the packages—Thanks loads. I guess ya best stop sending me stuff as I only have 18 to go and it might take me a month to finish or it might take me five—so by the time I receive the stuff that's on the way I might be done—who knows. I'm going to try to fly everyday—that is if they let me.

I received a letter from Cal yesterday and he says he is fine—I guess you know he is in France now and likes it much better than England. Kinda sorry to hear he is in combat so soon after getting there. I sure hope Joe gets his boys on the ball and make a running play for Berlin—all of us over here want Joe Stalin's boys to get there first and it looks like he will—if he gets there first—he'll make sure that Germany won't fight another war—ya can't soft soap him like the Allies.

I received all the pictures and they were all swell—you sure look good—and the kids—well they sure are beautiful. Mary Ellen is a cute kid and I'm sure Fred and her will be happy.

Hey! Lou want to do me another favor—Hell! I knew ya would—well! here's what I want you to do—I'm going to send home a cameo I bought in Naples and I want you to have it set in a necklace or some such thing—platinum setting to match Mel's rings—hang the cost just send me the bill. If ya like the cameo let me know and I'll send you—Ma and Boo Boo one. I sent Mel some gloves 12 or 13 pair and if you like them let me know the sizes of the women folk and I'll send a gross home. How much do kid's gloves cost back in the States? I paid $2.50–$2.75 and $4.00 for them—is that high?

Well! folks I guess I best close now—so loads of love and kisses to all of you.

Love
Dan

P.S. So ya finally beat the horses.

Calvin had left for the cold and misty plains of England in early May with other combat-inexperienced soldiers from the First Infantry Division. A group of seasoned veterans, hardened from their fighting in Africa, Sicily and Italy, launched Operation Overlord and had charged the beaches of Normandy on D-day. Calvin and his battalion had not been chosen for the great invasion but were quickly shipped as backup across the English Channel to the shores of Normandy.

Pa Joe wrote to Daniel:

Ma and I were terribly shocked that he [Cal] is in France. We figured he would at least get six months training in England before being sent into actual combat. It seems that Cal got every bad break since he left home. All we can do is go on praying that both you and he will weather the storm and come back to us just as good as when you left home.

Even during the summer months, northern France was cold and damp. Calvin wrote to his brother about the cold temperatures in Normandy: "I've got a pair of summer undies and a pair of wool undies, wool shirt, and fatigue suit along with a heavy field jacket and it's only the beginning of July."

"No doubt Cal has seen plenty of action by now and all we can do is pray that he and you will come through in good shape. All of us are well and praying that you two are tops," Pa Joe wrote to his bombardier.

The LaHurd family now had two boys facing death-defying odds every day across the pond.

Pa Joe wrote to his son in Sterparone:

> *Good morning to you my Honey Boy and best wishes for your health and safety. We keep closely informed on the air action out of Italy and of course the action in Normandy and sort of follow you and Cal in our minds. Ma and I are doing a very good job of keeping our chins up, so don't worry about us. Louise stays close to Ma during the day and we never leave her alone at night so we don't give her much time to be alone and have bad thoughts.*

To keep himself going during dangerous missions, Daniel often thought of Calvin and the other foot soldiers spread throughout the world, fighting day and night. He thought of the dirt and grime of living in foxholes, the rain and cold and the nights disturbed by the worry of looming surprise attacks. He also thought of the hell that Madeline must be going through back home, helplessly wondering how her husband was faring.

In early July, Pa Joe wrote:

> *Received a letter from Cal and as you already know he is on the fighting line in Normandy and I'm sweating each day and each mission out with you and Cal. I know damn fine it doesn't do any good to worry and keep fighting against it and think I'm doing a fairly good job. Sunday we took Mel to the noon Mass at St. Joseph...and lit a few candles for you and Cal.*

Rest camp in Naples had done Daniel some good, but he still couldn't manage to sleep through a full night since experiencing combat. Every time he closed his eyes to fall asleep, he'd remember a scene from a mission: an endless sea of exploding black clouds filling the sky from antiaircraft guns below, flak shaking his Fortress and engulfing the heavens with thunderous bursts or a friendly B-17 being torn to shreds by the enemy's weaponry. So many times, Daniel had helplessly watched in horror as bombers twirled to the ground, generating a trail of thick black smoke and debris, their fragments littering the sky as the once powerful planes flipped end over end.

Many of his fellow airmen never returned to Sterparone. LaHurd's emotions tended to get the best of him when the group returned with fewer bombers than the mission's start or when familiar faces were missing in the debriefing sessions, officers' club and at the poker table. Their absence confirmed that they were scattered across Europe, either imprisoned by the Nazi regime or dead. From the bomber's takeoff until its landing, death was literally and constantly just millimeters away.

The hike up the foothills of Foggia had taken Daniel about twenty-five minutes. He knew exactly where to go to find his favorite olive tree. He had made the trek a number of times before. His khaki pants, boots and green cotton T-shirt camouflaged him against the surrounding foliage. The locals who frequented these gradual slopes to prune what was left of their crops were off at Sunday worship. He was all alone to simply relax and think.

From his elevated perch, the view was breathtaking. Olive groves dotted the green slopes. In the valley below, meticulously tended grapevines and blotches of granaries dominated the lower grounds. Neglected dusty roads connected small villages. An occasional wooden fence jutted from the tall yellow grass, its purpose long forgotten. The natives below struggled every day to stay alive. Daniel had seen it firsthand. Women, children and the elderly spent their days searching for food. Benito Mussolini had sucked the country dry of its resources to feed and fuel his army. Weaponry from around the globe had leveled ancient towns and villages across Italy that had once been rich with history and beauty.

Daniel thanked the Lord for the luck he had had thus far. He wasn't completely convinced that someone was listening to him, but he felt it had taken an act of God for him to still be alive. The greatest feeling in the world was when his B-17's wheels touched the runway after a long, frigid and tense mission. And after he stepped out of his bombardier pod, stretched his legs and straightened his back, he appreciated that he was able to live another day, eat another meal, converse with his friends another night and write his family and lovely wife another letter.

Daniel's attention was drawn to his camp. Counting the tents off, he found his temporary home within the sea of erected canvases. It wasn't really all that difficult to recognize, considering it was the most identifiable and popular officers' tent on base. The entrance was designated by two large American flags flapping on improvised staffs manufactured from rusted metal poles. A hand-carved wooden sign christened the tent as LaHurd's Klassy Klip Klub.

Daniel had decided to keep Katz's club alive and functioning overseas. He considered it a franchise of Katz's original Klub back in Deming. The nylon walls and roof were held up by strategically placed wooden staffs. Ropes, tightly knotted, secured the fabric exterior. A small coal stove for cooking sat in the center of the tent, also providing heat to the four men who slept there: LaHurd, Smitty, Stegner and Kent.

The Klassy Klip Klub was only as orderly as it needed to be to meet compliance with senior officers. The tent's interior was filled with personal chests, cots and a circular oak table. Canned foods filled makeshift shelves throughout the living quarters. In early spring, LaHurd had traveled into town to purchase seven chairs, a coffeepot, a hat rack, washbowls, a washstand, candleholders and a chest of drawers. He and Smitty had personally torn up all the grass and weeds, leveled the ground inside and laid runway steel matting for the tent's flooring. LaHurd considered the sheets a loan from the AAF, but actually he had gone down to the flight line and stolen them.

He had written home about his Klub's progress: "We put an extension on the back end with a back door to it—put a wooden door in the front—white washed the inside…and all we need now is lights and music and I think by the time I get back to the tent from chow Smitty will have that."

The only real accommodation the tent lacked was plumbing.

Daniel's focus moved away from his tent to a group of B-17s just beneath the clouds making their gradual descent toward the runway. The bombers were returning to base from a mission somewhere over Europe. As he sat and watched his comrades from afar, he wondered how many more bases like Sterparone had been built around the world with military machinery ready to kill. How many soldiers, friend or foe, were dying around the world? How many families would receive a letter from their government telling them how admirably and courageously their son or husband had fought but failed to return home alive?

One by one, the assembly of B-17s began to touch down on the Italian landing strip. From this distance, the sounds of the massive engines were barely audible. Soft metal rings filled the air as church bells signaled noon and the conclusion of Mass. Daniel considered the irony of the rumbling engines of war and the clanging of peaceful church bells taking place simultaneously.

The first five bombers landed smoothly. The last bomber that had safely landed taxied off the runway as the next Fortress made its wobbly descent toward Earth. Thick black smoke billowed from one of its left wing engines, the obvious cause of the uncontrolled landing. Daniel watched intently as the right wheel smashed onto the ground, momentarily bouncing the aircraft airborne until the left wheel followed suit with a hard thump and piercing shriek. Daniel tensed, hoping the pilot could control the alternation of the banging wheels and bring the aircraft down safely. After a few more seconds of this whiplash, the plane leveled off, and the small tailwheel safely touched ground just as the left two engines engulfed in yellow flames. Black smoke quickly rose into the Italian sky like an active volcano. The men occupying the burning B-17 were lucky as they frantically exited the inferno through different escape hatches. What if luck wasn't so kind to Daniel on his next mission? His family would be devastated.

He looked up at the canopy of grayish-green that acted as a shelter from the afternoon sun and recalled hearing once that the leaves of the olive tree swaying in the breeze above him symbolized abundance, glory and peace. As he peered down at the airfield, he definitely saw abundance; abundance in the thousands of airmen, aircraft and weapons that made up the army air force base. He almost laughed when he thought of peace. This war seemed as though it would never end and peace would never return. At this moment, the olive tree that he leaned against was just a braided, disfigured tree reaching for the sky, symbolizing nothing.

Oftentimes, Daniel and Ryan had come to the tree to talk and plan their futures back home in New York and Ohio. Ryan had even considered moving to Akron after the war so that he could live closer to his buddy. They had become best friends, and the terrors of combat had seemed to bring them even closer together. Though Daniel's crew was like family, Ryan really did feel as close to him as his own brothers. They had so much in common— their comic wit; their taste in wine, women and cigars; their poker game; their willingness to engage in mischievous and crazy activities. Conversation between the two bombardiers came easily. Trips together to the olive tree or the city of Foggia were frequent, often accompanied by a large bottle of domestic Italian red wine and a pack of smokes. But from now on, Daniel's trips to the olive tree would be alone.

Two days earlier, Ryan's B-17 hadn't returned from its mission. LaHurd had stood at the end of the runway for nearly three hours watching for Ryan's bomber, smoking and waiting. Smitty came out to have a smoke with him. Daniel stood there, scanning the sky in search of a late bomber's arrival. He lingered in silence until the tobacco of his cigarette burned out.

Smitty had turned to him and said, "I've got a feeling they bailed out. That Ryan is a tough son-of-a-bitch. He probably found a nice little Slavic girl to shack up with until this war is over."

Daniel had grinned and hoped that Smitty's words held some truth.

Looking to the distance, gray clouds began to build over the white-capped sea. Daniel knew he had a good hike back to his Klassy Klip Klub. He closed his eyes, raised his chin and blindly looked to the Italian sky. He asked God to be with his best buddy. After hours of waiting on the runway that day, Daniel had learned from another crew that the bomber carrying Ryan had crashed into a mountain. Observers hadn't seen any parachutes. The crews had been flying to Ploesti on a bombing mission. The skies had been filled with flak. Ryan's bomber was hit and traveled southwest for miles until it entered a cloud. Poor visibility and damaged controls made for a deadly combination. The men were never seen again. They had all been killed in action. Daniel had lost his best friend.

Patting the large roots that seemed to swallow him, he said goodbye with a tear in his eye and headed down the hill back to Sterparone Airfield. In less than twenty-four hours, it would be time for him to begin the second leg of missions. Twenty-five more to go. The rumor drifting around the squadron was that their target would be somewhere in southern Germany.

Early the next morning, July 18, 1944, Daniel and his newly appointed pilot Smitty awoke to prepare for a critical bombing raid over southern Germany. The target: Memmingen Aerodrome.

Chapter 10

LAST REPOSE

July 18, 1944

*Your task will not be an easy one. Your enemy is well trained, well equipped and
battle hardened. He will fight savagely.*
—*General Dwight Eisenhower*

Time eerily slowed as LaHurd freefell through the icy cold air. The upward
draft smacked at his cheeks, causing small ice crystals to form over his
skin. His eyes were closed behind his goggles. The wind rushed over his
body, his right hand clinging to his parachute's D-ring. The fear of battle
had disappeared for a split second. The sounds and smells of war were gone.
He only saw darkness and only heard the rush of wind over his ears. The
moment was peaceful, surreal.

Though it had seemed like a lifetime of freefall, in reality it had been
barely four seconds. Daniel pulled the D-ring, causing his pilot chute to
project out into the air above him. The small chute opened and dragged
the massive piece of precision-folded nylon of the main chute out into the
atmosphere. As gravity pulled the bombardier's body toward earth, the
upward draft expanded the nylon and burst it open into a massive canopy.

The snap of Daniel's parachute kick-started his thought process. He
needed to survive. He needed to see Madeline again. He needed to tell his
mother and father that he was okay. On his slow and tortuous descent toward
Germany, he watched his plane erupt into a fireball as it hit the ground below.
Scanning the sky, he saw a number of parachutes gliding to the ground.
There was no way of knowing from this distance if the others were the crew

of *Virgil's Virgins*, but he sure as hell hoped they were. He then looked up to see a chilling sight: his buddies, members of the AAF, completely engaged in full-scale aerial warfare. The German fighters' devastating success made LaHurd grimace.

Debris rained down from above. Streaking contrails and blotches of black smoke blocked out sections of the blue sky. The battle above became blotches; the large, blurred dots headed in a straight line toward the determined target, while the smaller dots of enemy fighters moved in all directions, flipping and turning like energetic flies avoiding a swatter. Men continued to jump from their burning bombers, some with parachutes on fire and others with no parachutes at all. Four more Fortresses from the 817th went down in flames just after LaHurd jumped. Smoke, fire and chaos filled the sky.

The German *Luftwaffe* and *Wehrmacht* at Memmingen were in position to defend their base as warning sirens blared. The remaining B-17s and twelve long-awaited P-38 American fighters from the First Fighter Group coalesced over the aerodrome and installations to unleash a bombardment of exploding armament. The P-38s escorted the heavy bombers through a field of flagged enemy fighter planes and blankets of flak. The explosions of the surface-to-air artillery created shrapnel capable of slicing through steel. Black smoke from artillery explosions covered the sky. It was insane that anyone would willingly fly through these clouds of death, but the airmen knew it was necessary in order to get the job done.

The flak wasn't going to deter the Americans. There was no concealment for the Germans, as bombs from the Flying Fortresses began to devastate the entire area. According to the Intelligence Operations Summary, bomb strike photos showed

> *118 enemy aircraft present* [at Memmingen Aerodrome] *and of those 118 aircraft 17 enemy aircraft had been destroyed, 4 probably destroyed and 14 damaged.* A heavy concentration of strikes had covered the entire installations area on the north side of the Aerodrome. Two and possibly

---

* Of the 118 enemy aircraft present, 40 were single-engine aircraft, 77 were twin-engine aircraft and one was a multi-engine aircraft. Many years later, it was learned that the Me 262, the world's first jet fighter, was being built at an underground installation at Memmingen and an experimental prototype of the Me 264 was being tested. The latter, a four-engine, long-range bomber capable of reaching the United States, was destroyed on July 18, 1944, along with two more partially assembled prototypes and 80 percent of the production facilities.

three of the very large hangars had been very heavily hit and totally destroyed. Four other hangars on the north perimeter had suffered direct hits and damage by blasts. A very large hangar on the West boundary had received direct hits and near misses. Two warehouses and adjacent rolling stock in the south central part had suffered direct hits followed by fires and two explosions. Several small shops in the southeast corner had received direct hits and were destroyed. Scattered damage to shops, barracks and administration buildings in the west end of the area had also been visible.

In addition to the 35 destroyed and damaged enemy aircraft on the ground, another 66 enemy fighters had been destroyed by the gunners of the 483rd Bombardment Group in air-to-air combat. Of the original B-17s that had taken off on the morning of July 18, 1944, 26 bombers continued to Memmingen, and only 12 of those made it back to their bases in Italy. Against overwhelming odds, significant damage was done to the southern German base. With the loss of 101 enemy aircraft and the Memmingen Aerodrome in flames, the mission was accomplished.

But the calamity to the air force was devastating as well. The group lost fourteen B-17s, and 143 airmen were now either dead or missing in action.

The result of the 483rd's mission was a mystery to Daniel, who was about to land behind enemy lines.

LaHurd was at the mercy of the wind current. As his altitude slowly decreased, objects from the land below became clearer as they grew in size with each passing second. The once endless patches of farmland visible from his bombardier pod at twenty thousand feet became more concentrated. Just off to the east were small gray and brown cottages making up a tiny village and a long road. Outside the village, farmers had built barns, sheds and rustic farmhouses, now ramshackle and dilapidated. Cattle were contained by wooden fencing. Some sheep, goats and a few horses were discernible.

LaHurd scanned the sky. In the distance, he saw two other airmen falling to Earth. Suddenly, the villagers, men and children, rushed from shrubs and from barns into the fields with shovels, pitchforks, hoes, axes and hunting rifles toward the American airmen preparing to land. The locals' hatred for the bomber crews had been fueled by relentless German propaganda. Civilians had been fed horror stories of gangsters of the air (*luftgangsters*) and terror fliers (*terrorfliegers*). They had read in the papers about the fire bombings of Hamburg, and they had seen the massive bombers fly over their homes and cities. They had felt their bombs rumble the earth that they harvested. They had heard the screams and cries of their children and wives. The German civilians were known for taking their anger out on the captured airmen through hanging, stoning and beating. LaHurd watched as an airman safely hit the ground, tumbling to absorb the shock of his fall. Before the airman could unclip his parachute and get to his feet, a rush of angry civilians dashed toward him, their weapons held above their heads, ready to kill.

LaHurd finally came to a stop on a small farm. Thoughts of his family flashed in his head. How would he communicate to them? His mother would absolutely be devastated if something happened to him. His father would be proud that his son had died serving his country but would never fully recover from the death of one of his sons. And of course, his wife, his beautiful wife, would be waiting for him. He had promised her that he would see her again. He had done everything through his training and deployment to convince her and his family that the arduous military life and terrifying missions were anything but difficult and scary. How would he let them know he was okay?

The wind knocked out of him, disoriented and confused, he took a moment to return to reality. This repose was his last moment of freedom. In the distance, he could hear the faint sounds of aircraft engines roaring and buzzing. Barely audible gunfire and muffled pops from exploding planes echoed through the sky. Finally, taking his eyes off the maelstrom above and as the adrenaline slowed in his body, he felt wincing pain in his arms and chest. In the heat of battle, he never felt the small pieces of broken metal that had sliced through his skin. After unzipping his coat, he noticed bright red spots on his clothing. His handgun was nowhere to be found. But LaHurd's only concern was to get his parachute off, hide it as he had been trained to do and find some cover to contemplate his next move.

After wrestling with the pile of nylon and ropes that made up his parachute, he was free from the pack that had lowered him safely to the ground. The battle above had moved out of sight and could no longer be heard. His chute, snagged on a rock, flapped like a hooked fish as a slight breeze moved over the field. His sense of hearing had been impaired by battle noise, though he was still aware of an almost inaudible metal squeak over the pop of nylon and silk as the wind caught in small pockets of the discombobulated chute. Rolling over onto his belly, he saw a man yards away closing in fast through the mud. With nowhere to run, LaHurd rose to his knees to see that the man, in Nazi fatigues, was tossing a bicycle to the side of the dirt road and drawing a pistol from his waist. He began running toward LaHurd.

Wounded, the United States Army airman had little option but to kneel and listen uncomprehendingly to the screaming orders of the German. As the Nazi moved closer, LaHurd saw a massive scar stretching down the man's face. The German *unteroffizier*, now standing beside LaHurd, shouted and pointed his pistol at the exhausted American's head. Unable to understand the barking orders of his captor, the bombardier kneeled motionless in the mud, assuming he was going to be shot from point-blank range. His life was over. He couldn't believe it.

Mission number fifty and his free pass home never came. Mission number twenty-six, the Memmingen Raid, was his last. Overall, he had been lucky, pushing his odds. LaHurd had volunteered for every possible mission and bombed targets for four months. He had figured that the more he put his life on the line and the more missions he was a part of, the sooner he could get home. The incentive of seeing his wife and family was all he needed to risk his life twenty-six times. But that plan would not reach fruition. Reaching number twenty-six was no better than number ten or number five. He had needed to reach fifty. His family flashed through his thoughts. He prepared for his death.

LaHurd's captor raised him to his feet, still shouting orders in his native tongue. The ensuing march was a long and painful one. The expected bullet to the head never came, though the countless thrusts of the Luger occasionally made contact with the back of the American's head. Marching through the mud, the two men, American and German, prisoner and Nazi, played a game of punch and duck. The bombardier looked like a boxer weaving away from the painful blows. LaHurd was now a prisoner of war under Nazi Germany.

Chapter 11

NAZI INTERVIEW

July 18, 1944–July 28, 1944

If you are going through hell, keep going.
—Prime Minister Winston Churchill

The intervals between the thrusts and swings of the Luger to the lieutenant's head seemed to grow further apart the longer they marched. Small lumps had already begun to protrude from his scalp. LaHurd's boots were caked in mud. The wet, soggy ground stuck to the bottom of his treaded soles, throwing his center of gravity off with every step. The clumps of mud created a difficult walking surface for his already weakened legs, and it seemed as though every ten steps were followed by a twisted ankle. Every time the POW's pace slowed, the *unteroffizier* shoved the barrel of his gun deep into LaHurd's kidneys, driving pain through his already injured body. The soreness in his chest was excruciating. His shirt, torn open and stained with a mixture of blood and mud, chafed at his shrapnel wounds. Through his misery, he did notice a series of distant rumbles echoing across the landscape, confirmation that the remaining B-17s of the 483rd Group had made it to Memmingen Aerodrome.

The storm had moved through the German foothills hours ago. The sun was desperately attempting to evaporate the watery mess that had been unleashed earlier in the morning. The humid air stuck to LaHurd's body, and the afternoon sunshine beamed down on his face. Mud on his sleeves and hands slowly started to dry, forming a cracking surface of thick dirt. The captured lieutenant cautiously surveyed his surroundings, trying to find an escape. There was nowhere to run and nowhere to hide.

Nearly the entire group of airmen that had bailed out on the mission was captured immediately and was eventually rounded up within an hour. A few remained free for a week, making it all the way to the borders of Switzerland, only to be blocked by Lake Constance and the German border patrols.

The lieutenant and the *unteroffizier* were approaching a group of men. Two odd-looking jeeps with sloped hoods sat parked on the side of the road. As the distance between the two parties closed, LaHurd saw that there were captured Americans huddled in a circle on the side of the road closely guarded by enemy soldiers. A few locals with pitchforks in hand stood nearby, yelling at the captured men. Two Alsatians, desperately trying to break free from their masters' tight grip, lunged toward the American airmen. The K-9s' growls and barks echoed over the open fields.

Although LaHurd still had no idea if he was going to be shot or tortured, he felt some relief knowing he had Americans with him. As he approached the group, he quickly recognized Sergeant John Papamanoli, the right waist gunner of *Virgil's Virgins*.

LaHurd's voice was coarse from dehydration and fear, but he managed to exhale a sentence to his comrades: "Damn am I glad to see some real soldiers."

The Nazis didn't know exactly what the American said, but still LaHurd was punched in the kidney by his scarred captor and screamed at in German. This immediately silenced the prisoners, and their grins quickly faded. Papamanoli stealthily winked at Daniel, acknowledging his comment. The group marched together under the German afternoon sun. Hours later, a small town appeared at the horizon.

LaHurd's chest continued to seep blood. One of the other American airmen, unknown to the bombardier, noticed LaHurd's weakened state and decided to tend his wounds. Again, the Nazis screamed and the dogs began to bark. But they didn't push the two Americans apart. They allowed the largest wound to be bandaged up with materials from the airman's first aid kit. After the attention to his wound, LaHurd's weight was bolstered by the stranger.

They hiked from the crash site, nineteen miles south of Memmingen just off Highway Aichstetten, to the Bavarian city of Kempten. Here the captives were forced into a barn where two other Americans sitting on haystacks had already been locked inside. All of their faces were covered in dirt, soot and burnt gunpowder from the morning's airstrike. Their hair was sweaty and messy. They looked like homeless men in their tattered and muddied clothes. The two airmen, a bombardier and a gunner, created space on the haystacks for the wounded bombardier. LaHurd collapsed onto the improvised bedding. The American prisoners greeted one another with half-strained smiles and handshakes. The doors to the barn slammed shut, and the clanging of metal chains assured the Americans that they were locked in.

Wincing, LaHurd asked an obviously exhausted Papamanoli, "How'd our crew fare? Did everyone get out of the plane?"

After a brief pause and a shake of the head, Papamanoli replied, "Davenport didn't make it out." He paused to collect his emotions. "He was slumped over his gun when I bailed. Poor guy was torn to hell from shrapnel. He was a good man, sir."

The gunners on the mission had been replacements. LaHurd didn't know them. His first time meeting them had been earlier in the morning before takeoff. All the gunners' faces that morning had looked so young to the bombardier. LaHurd sat there and shook his head, ashamed of what the war was doing.

Papamanoli continued, "The other guys in the back made it out okay. Marlin was ripped up pretty bad. His legs and arms were a mess. Shrapnel got him too."

LaHurd was glad to hear that everyone else made it out okay. He knew the navigator, engineer and copilot had made it out because they had headed for the same open hatch as LaHurd. His real concern was the well-being of his buddy Smitty. Smitty was making his way down to the hatch as LaHurd dropped from the plane. LaHurd had assumed Smitty made it out, but he couldn't be sure. He prayed that his pilot was safe.

The inside of the barn was damp and had a mixed smell of manure and dry, dusty grain. Slices of sunlight snuck through multiple cracks in the rotting wood panels of the exterior walls. There were big enough gaps between the panels of wood for the captured airmen to peek outside, but all they could see was a small village road and the side of an adjacent stone building.

The group of POWs searched the interior for something to use as a weapon in case the Nazis came back with murder on their minds. Empty metal hooks dotted the wooden beams where farm equipment had once hung. The ground was a mixture of dirt and straw. There was a loft above but no ladder to gain access. The guards must have stripped the inside clean before using the barn as a holding cell. LaHurd had noticed on his march in that the loft door was boarded up from the outside.

The Americans quietly identified themselves to one another. They had all traveled from Italy with the same mission: destroy Memmingen. With conversation at a whisper, the men briefly went over their personal morning's scenario and capture. Each bomber had its own designated hangar, airstrip, repair shed, barracks or railroad track to bomb. Most of the details were left out of the conversation, as the men didn't know who was listening just outside the barn. Also, these men didn't really know one another, and the Germans were known to put spies in prison camps to gain information. LaHurd and Papamanoli agreed to keep their close ties a secret from the Germans for as long as possible to avoid permanent separation and threats of torturing one to get answers from the other.

The prisoners had to simply sit and wait, letting fate take its course. Each man was physically exhausted, but the current predicament failed to allow their minds to relax. None of them knew what was next. Where would they be sent? Would they be tortured? Would they be murdered?

Daniel held an open palm to his chest wound. He closed his eyes and prayed that he would see his wife. He prayed for his brother Calvin. He prayed that the news of his downed plane wouldn't overwhelm his father and mother.

The chains outside clanged and the rusty hinges squeaked as the large wooden doors swung open. Two Nazis stood in the entrance with the butts of their rifles tucked tightly into their shoulders, their cross hairs aimed at the POWs. A third man, armed with a Luger, entered the barn. He was tall and slender. His chest was accentuated by the tight gray jacket that he wore. With a straight face, he pointed at the prisoners and said in twisted English, "If any ohv you reeesist or cause me trohble you vill be shot."

With the muzzle of his gun, the German pointed at the airman sitting next to Daniel and ordered, "You come vith me." The gunner stood and unsteadily walked from the barn, unsure if death awaited him outside.

A low-level amateur interrogator performed the interrogations at Kempten. One by one, the men were taken from the barn to a vacant cellar beneath the village's inn. Threatening death and torture, the interrogator pressed for any information regarding the Americans' mission. The POWs were enticed with cigarettes, medical attention for their wounds, new clothes, fresh food and information about their missing crew members. Alternately, the interrogator threatened to open scabbed wounds or kill fellow prisoners. All these techniques proved unsuccessful, as each airman only revealed his name, rank and serial number.

After each airman spent approximately an hour in the dank cellar with the Nazi, he was released back into the barn or, if injured, taken to the local doctor, who reluctantly tended to his wounds. The trip to and from the cellar was more frightening than the interrogation itself. The guard's duty changed from keeping the Americans from escaping to keeping the

Americans alive. The local citizens of the small southern town loathed the Allied air forces. The seemingly untouchable planes from high above were leveling their ancient cities, destroying their crops, killing their family members. The citizens of Kempten tried to attack the POWs with pitchforks, shovels, rocks and knives—anything that could be used as a weapon. Though they did not understand the locals' furious screams and shouts, the Americans didn't need a translator to recognize the sheer hatred coming from the angry mobs.

LaHurd and the other POWs lived in the Kempten barn for two days, traveling back to the cellar for more interrogation every few hours. The city's civilians heckled and tormented the men with each trip. On July 20, the American prisoners were packed into a boxcar already filled with other Allied prisoners. The boxcar was attached to a German military train. The roof had been painted with large white letters designating that the link in the train held prisoners of war. From Kempten, the train traveled 281 miles to Frankfurt. The long trip lacked bathrooms, food and seats. Bouncing Betty had been a luxurious first-class locomotive in comparison to this crammed boxcar. At Frankfurt, the POWs were placed in trolleys and taken to Dulag Luft* in Wetzlar, where they officially came under the control of the *Luftwaffe*. Although his future was unknown and the days ahead would be filled with further interrogation, fear and discomfort, LaHurd was thankful that he had managed to avoid the angry civilians, German Waffen-SS and the Gestapo. The men of the *Luftwaffe* had a general respect for the men of the army air force, and more importantly, the *Luftwaffe* frequently obeyed the laws of the Geneva Accords. The Waffen-SS, Gestapo and the locals followed few international laws.

Dulag Luft was encircled in twelve-foot-high fencing capped with razor-sharp barbed wire. Regularly spaced placements of guard towers and pillboxes ensured the interrogators that their prisoners were safely locked within. Guards and their dogs routinely and thoroughly investigated every square foot of the camp as they maneuvered around large white painted rocks. Bombardiers and fighter pilots from high above were the only individuals capable of understanding the true purpose of the white rocks, whose alignment spelled out "POW." The rooftops of the barracks were also painted with the three bold white letters. This was the only designation that provided the Nazis safety from aerial assaults.

---

* The English translation of *Dulag Luft*, short for *Durchgangslager der Luftwaffe*, is "transit camp of the air force."

Unshaven, filthy and exhausted, LaHurd stood naked on a cold concrete floor while Nazi guards searched his body. An Alsatian guard dog sniffed at the prisoner's uniform that lay in a wrinkled pile on the floor. White bandages covered most of his chest. The rank smell of body odor emanated from his skin. His belly gurgled from hunger, his mouth dry from thirst. Embarrassment and discomfort toyed with his morale. It was just the beginning of his interrogation session at the German facility. He had already been searched a number of times since his capture, and he realized this was more of a mental breach, a mind game, than a security inspection. After the long, uncomfortable search, the guards returned his clothing, and he dressed quickly.

After his strip search, the lieutenant was placed into a small concrete cell no bigger than a walk-in closet. His cell was one of many that lined either side of a long concrete corridor. The cramped confine was damp and depressing. A small puddle had formed in the back corner from a monotonous drip that leaked through the cracked ceiling above. The cell was empty except for a rickety wooden bed frame holding a thin, burlap mattress stuffed with hay. A small barred window allowed for some natural light to sneak in.

LaHurd was exhausted. His weakened body collapsed onto the bedding as the cell door slammed shut and the guard's boots clipped down the corridor. The condition of Daniel's small room hardly registered in his tired mind. He was too worn out to make any observations. The lice that crept over his filthy bed made no difference, nor did the abrasive material of his mattress that scratched at his skin. He lay there completely drained of any physical or mental strength. But he couldn't fall asleep. Exhaustion couldn't overcome the fear of his unknown future. The minutes slowly moved to hours and the hours dragged into days. LaHurd found some sleep, mainly drifting in and out of consciousness.

The food, if one could call it that, was a tasteless, dry mix of dirt, sawdust, sand and wheat made up into a blackish-tan bread. This served as breakfast and dinner. Water was scarce, and lunch only differed from the other two meals with an addition of maggot-filled soup.

The mental torment was excruciating. Hour after hour of tormenting boredom dragged on. The uncertainty of his situation was the worst part. He had no idea what was in store for him—torture or even death. He didn't know how long he would be held in this cell—days, months or years. He didn't even know if there would be a tomorrow. He prayed that he would see his Madeline again. Just one more kiss, one more hug. The thought of her kept him going.

After two days of solitary confinement, the time had come for the lieutenant's weakened mind and body to meet the interrogators. These interrogators were highly skilled in comparison to the amateurs at Kempten. Their English was fluent. Their knowledge of America, the Fifteenth Air Force, even the 817th Squadron was surprisingly thorough. They were trained to quickly learn and understand the POW's fears, desires, comforts and discomforts.

Daniel revealed his name, rank and serial number—nothing more. The only useful information he actually held back was that his intent a few days earlier had been to pummel Memmingen. But he assumed this was obvious, as Allied bombs had rained down on the aerodrome on July 18. He didn't know what his next mission was going to be. There wasn't much information for him to give.

After interrogation, he was escorted back to his humid cell, where he sat and contemplated worst-case scenarios. Each passing minute brought more uncertainty. To occupy the time and quiet his mind, he decided to add some art to the cell walls that were filled with etched sentences, phrases, quotes and drawings from past prisoners. Most of the graffiti was used to release anger toward Hitler and the Nazis. Other phrases were encouraging words about America or the Allies' looming victory. LaHurd's favorite line was scratched into the wall just above the head of the bed: "Hang in there PAL."

A small sliver of tarnished metal, no bigger than a thumbtack, was lodged into the treaded rubber sole of LaHurd's boot. After wiggling it free, he used the piece of scrap as an improvised chisel and worked at the wall parallel to his bunk. After a half hour, the first two capital letters were complete: "ED."

A guard's boots echoed down the corridor, stopping at LaHurd's cell. It was time for his visit to the bathroom. The prisoners were granted only one bathroom visit a day. He poked the piece of metal into his burlap mattress, hiding it from the guard. Daniel had no idea what the punishment would be for defacing Nazi property, and he didn't want to find out.

After relieving himself, his tender fingers were back to etching. His fingertips became raw. His attention to detail slowly waned as the hours passed. The first three letters were heavily bolded and dug deep into the concrete. The following letters were lighter, not so straight, not so detailed: "EDBTZ Hitler." The phrase, "Your hand is up your ass," said in Arabic, sounded distinctly similar to saying the letters "E, D, B, T, Z" quickly in English. Hence the translation of his code: "Your hand is up your ass, Hitler." He didn't have to worry about the guards deciphering the five letters and punishing him for the derogatory comment toward their Führer.

While Daniel bounced around Germany as a prisoner of war, his family had no idea that he had been captured. For all they knew, he was still living in Sterparone and flying missions. Their most recent letters from Akron to Italy had never reached Daniel, and weeks into August, those letters were returned to 1099 Berwin Street.

July 29, 1944
Akron, Ohio

Dear Dan;

Ma just called and said three letters came from Cal. Don't know whats in them but will let you know in my next letter. Well this is near the end of July and also near the finish for Hitler. If the Russians can keep up their present pace for two more weeks, they will be inside Germany which would force the Nazis to ue for peace. Today, sent you 1 box of O'Henry Bars and 6 Jars of Pineapple, cheese. I'd like to send some canned fruits but will have to wait until the new pack comes in as there is no stock on hand now. Last night Ma and I visited the neighbors and at 11 p.m. we started a four handed game of dealers choice poker or milk the crew and I was $40.00 to the good when the game broke up at 1 a.m. as we had agreed to do. Mike was in here, the office, a bit ago and says a cheery hello to you. It looks like the two St. Louis teams will battle it out during the World Series, the "Browns" are 3½ games to the good and the Cardinals are making a runaway of it with a 14½ game lead, they are a sure cinch but the "Browns" may falter and lose out. All well and pray your tops in every way.

Love + Kisses
Mother + Dad
XXXXXXX

July 31, 1944
Akron, Ohio

Dear Dan;

We went to church with Mel and the F. LaHurds and met the M. LaHurd's with their children and Lou and Mary Lou, so you see this war has made us think of God and his blessings. We had dinner at our house and enjoyed having the family together. Went home for lunch today more to find a letter from you but no luck, hope to get one this week. I am enclosing one letter from Cal, which came Saturday. You'll note he hasn't received mail from us in six weeks. I called the Red Cross about the delay and they said the Army couldn't set up post offices fast enough to make prompt deliveries and suggested that I send him a cablegram to assure him we are well. I called the Western Union and they checked his A.P.O. number and said they could get a message to him, so I'm going to do so after I finish this letter. War news continues good, in this mornings Plain Dealer *I read that the Russians are seven miles in East Russia and that the General in command is a few. You can bet he won't show them any mercy. It is just about a year ago that you and Cal came home. The following Sunday, Aug. 13th I'm having High mass for you and Cal. Ma and I will make a pilgrimage to Our Lady of Consolation in Carey, Ohio on Aug. 15th which is her Holy Day and pray for our two soldier boys, that they may return home to us. Mel is going along. All well and hope you are alright in every way.*

Love + Kisses
Mother + Dad
XXXXXXX

July 17, 1944

Dear Folks

Today was a real summer day. The sky was blue and the sun shone bright and warm as ever. The surprise of the day was when they took us out for warm showers. The first one in France and I sure did enjoy it. Now I'm all cleaned up and feel about ten pounds lighter. I also washed a few of my clothes and they are already dried out. Please don't worry about me for I'm sage and really having an experience of seeing many exciting things.

Please don't ever send me money or clothes for I have plenty of both. Just write everyday and don't get worried if I don't write often. Be good and be happy.

Love
Cal

Aug. 1, 1944
Akron, Ohio

Dear Dan;

We are going to Mike's tonight as it is Beulah's birthday. Ma got her a silk slip and I bought a nice card to go with it. The main topic of any conversation most everywhere is "when will the war end." There are all kinds of predictions and the best yet from an optimistic viewpoint is

that it will end this coming Friday, Aug. 4th which is too good to come true. Nevertheless, the end is not far off, as the Nazis are bound to crack soon under the terrific pounding they are being subjected to. I can hardly wait to hear how many missions you have had. Today I sent you a 2 lb Fruit Cake and 1½ lbs. of Hard Candy from Kaaser in one pkg. and 12—4½ cans of Clapps Stained Peaches which is put up for babies but I figured it might please you as you no doubt are hungry for canned peaches. Let me know if it's O.K. and I'll continue to send more, at least until the new crop canned fruit comes in. Have you had any news on Ryan. The Ponies are coming to Thistledown Wed. Aug 9th and will stay thru Labor Day, 24 days of excitement which I hope will be profitable for me. All of us are feeling well and hope your tops.

Love + Kisses
Mother + Dad
XXXXXXX

The lieutenant spent a miserable seven days at Dulag Luft, with days of solitary confinement and then hours of interrogation followed by days of confinement and more interrogation. This maliciously repetitive routine pulled at his brain until he was finally released from the camp on July 28. He and other American POWs were stripped of their flying equipment— boots, jackets and suits—placed in trolleys and taxied back to Frankfurt, where they awaited another POW train that would take them to their final destination: *Stalag Luft I.*

Chapter 12

THE DASH

July 24, 1944–July 25, 1944

Bravery is the capacity to perform properly even when scared half to death.
—General Omar Bradley

Hundreds of POWs stood in line for morning roll call behind the gates of the prison camp. The Allied captives within their individual compounds were encircled by parallel barbed wire fences of fifteen feet separated by a four-foot strip of soil. Every one hundred feet, guard towers supporting machine guns and spotlights had been erected around the camp. The guards in the towers constantly kept a cautious eye on the activity inside the camp and any movement outside the fences. Guard dogs, ferocious Alsatians, surveyed the perimeter in an attempt to pick up the scent of an escape tunnel. Guards inside pillboxes and men on foot patrol held submachine guns and rifles, their eyes searching for any out-of-the-ordinary behavior.

A layer of grimy dust topped the expanse of packed and dried mud. On dry, breezy days, the dust clogged the air. The loose joints and drafty windows of the ramshackle barracks allowed the clouds of particles to blow into the living quarters and settle onto and into everything. On rainy days, the saturated earth quickly became a stretch of mud dotted with pools of mucky water. Leaking latrines would diffuse throughout the grounds and give off a putrid smell of human waste.

As the ranking American officer hollered off the surrounding prisoners' names, Nazi guards looked on, hopeful that a determined captive would make a run for freedom. The guards were eager to fire their guns to kill the Allies.

As the officer neared the middle of the list, he found his way to the Ls. "Ladd!" he hollered.

"Sir," replied the private as he stepped forward.

"Laffante!"

"Sir," called the corporal.

"LaHurd!"

"Sir," yelled the army private from the first infantry, as all the other POWs had done.

Three days earlier, on July 25, a Panzer division in northwest France near Saint Lô had captured Private Calvin LaHurd.

The Allied forces started to build up on the beaches of Normandy after the battles of D-day on June 6. Over a month had gone by since the massive armada attacked the beachhead. The offensive push by the Allies was slow, and the drive into France was behind schedule. The Allied forces were like a shaken bottle of soda: ready to blow, ready to fight. All someone needed to do was pop the cap and release the pressure. By July 23, the Allies had amassed nearly 1.4 million soldiers in Normandy. The hedgerow fighting made a push sluggish and difficult. The lines of hedges and small trees endemic to the region acted as natural blockades that were perfect for hiding Nazi soldiers and tanks and formed dangerously narrow passageways for U.S. Sherman tanks.

The month of July 1944 was the rainiest month for Normandy in nearly forty years. Weather and logistics had delayed the "Dash Across France," and the Allied troops waited for orders on the beaches of the North Sea. Those orders finally came from General Omar Bradley. Operation Cobra was given the go-ahead for July 24. But the battle was delayed for another twenty-four hours due to weather. To the dismay and fury of the Allied generals, a bevy of Allied bombers from the Eighth Air Force didn't receive the delay orders and continued on with the initial strike date of July 24. Blinded by the rain clouds and fog, these bombers dropped their ordnance onto Allied positions. The Allied troops at the frontlines were shellshocked and dazed. Twenty-seven soldiers were killed, and another 131 were wounded.

General Bradley stuck to his plan and decided to continue on with July 25, refusing to let the staggered front lines delay the push any longer. He knew it was vital for the Allies to get out of the bocage as soon as possible and hit the open country to the south.

On the morning of July 25, the fight began. Operation Cobra was underway, and the Allies started their main offensive push into France from the outskirts of St. Lô.

The soggy ground dampened Calvin's combat uniform. Lying on his chest, face buried into the earth, he struggled to find oxygen as mud filled his left nostril. He used a fallen tree as cover from the bullets winging overhead. Men's screams were drowned out by exploding mortars, aerial bombs and the blasts of tank guns. This was the beginning of "The Dash."

Calvin couldn't lift his head. His adversaries had his location pinpointed. Their enfilades of bullets kept him pinned down as they chewed away at the bark of the tree that sat between him and the enemy. He did what he could to peek around the base of the tree where the displaced roots reached into the air. The eighty-year-old hunk of wood, probably blown from the earth during the air raid the day before, looked as though a giant had torn it from the ground and thrown it onto its side.

A few well-placed shots from Calvin's M1 semi-automatic rifle caused the Nazis across the field to take cover. His gun's chamber pinged with each squeeze of the trigger. The empty shells discharged onto the soil around his muddy combat boots. The rifle's recoil punched at his shoulder. For the most part, Calvin was firing at the muzzle flashes from his enemy's guns. The confusion was indescribable. Forming up and taking aim at somebody was nearly impossible. So Calvin just fired.

Down the German line, out of his range, he could see two Nazis partially exposed from behind a hedgerow, preparing to fire their rocket tank rifle. The foes nicknamed this weapon *Ofenrohr*—stovepipe. The exhaust from the *Ofenrohr* blasted out the back of the barrel, and seconds later, a massive explosion erupted to the left of Calvin's position. His view was blocked by another line of hedgerows, but he knew by the sound that an M4 Sherman had been hit. Multiple pops and crackles followed the larger explosion. The Sherman's artillery inside had caught fire and was exploding. The unfortunate crew within were instantly cremated.

Seconds later, the Nazis' position erupted into a fireball from an Allied shell. Dirt and rock blew into the air. The *Ofenrohr*, now a disfigured piece of pipe, flew fifty feet into the sky before crashing to the ground. The two adversaries' bodies exploded into a cloud of flesh and bones.

Twenty feet down the tree from where Calvin lay, an unknown soldier found cover. The soldier's body was squeezed between the split of two large branches. Dirt and debris flew in all directions as bullets and mortars continued to hit the surrounding area. The air was filled with smoke and dust. Visibility was limited. The soldier was armed with a British Lanchester submachine gun. How the American got the gun Calvin would never know. The Lanchester rattled off a round of bullets through the leafed branches and into the German front. A grayish smoke rose from the hot muzzle of the British gun.

The rumbling of B-17 engines could be heard as they came in high above from the north. The explosions of their armament soon drowned out their engines' noise. Bombs fell so close to Calvin's position that he was lifted off the ground from the shockwaves. He flipped around like a rag doll. Trees, tanks and men were blown from the earth, hurled into the sky and dropped like toys. Some of the bombs haplessly fell behind friendly lines, taking the lives of many of Calvin's comrades.

As the wave of bombers emptied their hulls and cleared the airspace for the next bevy, there was a brief lull in the action. A short duration of silence fell over the battlefield, interrupted by distant screams and even more distant artillery explosions. The settling of blast debris trickled to the ground like a light rain. The bark of a distant dog echoed through the trees.

The recess in action allowed Calvin to reestablish his bearings and blindly fire a few rounds over the tree's trunk in the direction of the enemy. A muffled sound engulfed his ears, and the thumping of his heart pounded at his rattled brain. Slowly, soldiers regained their bearings, and the battle escalated from the popping of single guns to the full-fledged battle it had been before the Allied bombers arrived. The air quickly became saturated with a torrent of bullets and cannon fire.

A line of hedgerows ran just to the west of Calvin's position. His eyes burned from dirt and discharged gunpowder. Through the hazy air, he could see an Allied M4 Sherman tank positioned in a split in the hedgerow, its .50-caliber gun spraying a cloud of bullets into the enemy. A group of Allied infantrymen peeked around the rear of the tank, adding to the carnage with their rifles and machine guns. Calvin wanted to get the hell out of his position and regroup with his men.

Lying on his belly, the soldier sharing Calvin's cover unleashed another fury of bullets at the Nazis. Seconds later, a German Panzer IV parked nearly five hundred meters from the Allied front lines fired a shell that tore through the tree, lifting the massive maple off the ground. Calvin wiped the mud from his face, shook the dirt and woodchips from his helmet and whipped around on his side to check on the soldier. A smoldering crater now replaced the root of the tree along with the soldier hiding behind it. Dirt and smoke slowly settled to the ground. The soldier's Lanchester submachine gun lay mangled only inches from Calvin's foot, half an arm still clinging to the side of the gun.

The artillery's explosion caused the tree to roll, exposing Calvin to the enemy. He had to crouch even flatter than before. His right side pressed up tightly against the tree. He couldn't get any closer. He needed to make a run for the Sherman.

Reaching over the trunk with his rifle, he blindly emptied his clip into the foliage across the field. He crawled on his hands and knees, still tightly tucked next to his barrier, and reloaded his rifle. Explosions erupted all over the battlefield. Bullets whizzed by as Nazis and Allies exchanged fire. He prepared for the fifty-yard dash to his comrades across the open expanse. The Sherman was guaranteed to give him more protection than his rifle, and he'd have men to watch his back.

A jeep sat in the middle of the field between Calvin and the Sherman, billowing black smoke high into the air as small flames ate away at the rubber tires. Stray bullets occasionally ricocheted off the body of the immobilized vehicle. Two American infantrymen lay dead around the smoldering jeep; another soldier hung lifelessly out of its back. Calvin could use the wreckage as cover, regain his composure, lay down some more cover fire and scurry to the tank.

The moss and damp ground under his feet made it difficult to get footing for a good push. He couldn't rise to his feet until he was ready to run. If he stood, he'd be target practice. The ground was slick. Adrenaline surged through his muscles and fed his tired legs. He popped from his wooden barrier and made his dash over the cratered earth. The Germans called the land *mondlandshaft*, lunar landscape. The American soldiers from behind the Sherman spotted Calvin's attempt, and they instinctively laid down a barrage of cover fire, momentarily pinning the Nazis down. Halfway to his destination, halfway to the steel and 75mm gun of the Sherman, the B-17s made another bombing run. He could hear their roaring engines growing louder overhead. Soon after, the bombs began to explode.

The blasts were so powerful and so close that they picked Calvin off the ground and tossed him through the air. He was at the mercy of their shockwaves. His ears throbbed from the deafening explosions. His eyes burned from the debris and fumes. Another bomb, and another, and another, tossed and turned him. They were so close. They were too close.

Darkness took over. He lay unconscious in the open terrain. The American tank, only minutes ago firing shells into the enemy's line, was now an inferno of molten steel. The hatch was twisted open. Flames and black smoke billowed. The white star painted across its side was now covered in charred grayish black soot. The Allies lay scattered around the area, either dead or wounded. Screams of pain echoed through the fields. The lucky few who had avoided the shrapnel and deadly shockwave were knocked out from the blasts.

The B-17s' heavy bombs managed to perform extreme destruction on the enemy but mistakenly delivered the same blow to the Americans. The Allied front lines were stunned and bewildered. The aerial armada of 1,507 bombers killed 111 soldiers and wounded over 500 more.

Calvin and fifteen other men in his general area had been cut off from their division by the Allied bombing run. The surviving Nazis cautiously advanced toward the discombobulated American group. Private Calvin LaHurd awoke to the bumpy ride of a cargo truck transporting him and other Allied prisoners to interrogation. He, like his brother Daniel, was now a prisoner of war. The ride from the outskirts of St. Lô, away from the front lines and deep into France, was an uncomfortably long one. The Nazi truck, packed with a dozen prisoners and a handful of armed *Wehrmacht*, traveled down cratered roads and over the rubble of ancient buildings. Calvin's head felt as though it was going to explode from the morning's shockwaves. He looked at the boyish faces sitting around him. The average age was probably twenty years old. They were all exhausted. Their eyes were heavy, their faces filthy, their skin colorless. A stream of dried blood traveled from the hairline of one soldier down his face, down his neck and disappeared underneath his shredded khaki jacket. Another soldier's ears were filled with clotted blood. His eardrums were almost certainly destroyed.

The breakthrough at St. Lô was a thrashing success for the Allies. After breaking free of the hedgerows at Normandy, the Allies led by General Patton's newly formed Third Army began to push through France, making up for the lost time between June 6 and July 25. They would soon be knocking on the gates of Paris.

But this advance was unknown to Calvin and his comrades on the truck. The realization that he was a prisoner began to sink in. His head throbbed, and the uncertainty of his future only added to his growing migraine.

As Calvin bounced through France on his long journey to Stalag VII in Moosburg, Germany, Daniel's interrogation was concluding at Dulag Luft.

Chapter 13

STALAG LUFT I

July 28, 1944–July 31, 1944

Maybe this world is another planet's Hell.
—Aldous Huxley

The guarded perimeter and dismal surroundings of Daniel's prison was comparable to that of Calvin's stalag. A collection of wooden barracks sat in rows within razor-crowned fencing. Outside the wire fences to the west lay a deep forest of pines. On occasions when the wind was just right, the fresh aroma of sap and moist pine needles masked the usual smells of mildew, human waste and body odor. The remainder of the time, the winds came from the northeast off the Baltic Sea and often brought gray clouds along.

Situated in the far northern lands of Germany, *Stalag Luft I* rarely reached temperatures above sixty-five degrees in the summer and became bitterly cold in the winter, with heavy snow and blizzard-like conditions. The damp, soggy ground, a perfect natural deterrent for tunnel building, became rock solid in the winter months as freezing temperatures blew through. The barracks, stilted four feet off the land, were refrigerated from the arctic winds blowing above and below it like an icy bridge. In the winter months, daylight spanned only six hours at such a high latitude. During the summer months, the sun was up until almost midnight.

Outside the city of Barth, Daniel LaHurd waited to exit a boxcar, one of many making up the German train that had transported prisoners and other Nazi commodities from Frankfurt to this fishing village off the Baltic

Sea. The ride had been a long and miserable one. The officers had been packed into one-half of the car. Five German guards occupied the other half. Sleeping had been next to impossible due to the humidity, stench and restricted space. The guards had sat around a table on crates with enough room to walk around or lie down. The inside of the car was dark and humid. Daniel was forced to take deep breaths to gain a sufficient amount of oxygen through the thick, dusty air. Scattered straws of hay overlapped one another, partially covering the wooden planked floor.

The prisoners were dazed, disoriented and partially blinded by the daylight as the boxcar doors slid open. One by one, the prisoners slowly hopped from the car. Outside their rolling jail cell, the damp Baltic Sea air was a welcome relief from the smells of sweat, rotting wounds and human waste that had filled the car during the three-day journey.

LaHurd's body ached. He cracked his neck. The pops trickled down his spine, stopping between his shoulder blades. He stretched his legs, and again the tension in his lower back was relieved by a pop. As he jumped from the car's open door, his blistered and bruised feet sent pain signals to his brain. One after another, prisoners continued to hop from boxcars while Nazi guards began lining up the captives in the train yard for their long march ahead.

LaHurd and the others had no idea what to expect from the stalag. Each man had his own vision of what the Germans offered as a prison camp. All Daniel could think about was getting his hands on some food and a cigarette and taking a long, warm shower. The thought of spaghetti, garlic bread and a glass of Chianti preoccupied his imagination. He'd do almost anything to be back in Foggia eating homemade pasta with Ryan—the forkful of knotted noodles dripping red meat sauce down his chin and the slight tingle of fermented grapes warming his throat. The thought quickly disintegrated as his stomach angrily grumbled like the puttering of a car engine running out of fuel. He had essentially been fed scraps for the past two weeks, and the scant number of calories was taking a toll on his body.

The walk through the town of Barth to *Stalag Luft I* loosened up his joints a bit, but his weak and hungry muscles found each step to be a challenge. Under his stained and reeking shirt were his bacteria-infested bandages. The surface of his scabbed wounds itched like a nagging rash. Looking around at some of the other officers, he felt fortunate that his injuries were not life threatening. Their conditions almost made him feel healthy. An officer to LaHurd's right was on crutches. A pair of men walking in front of LaHurd had bloodied bandages wrapped around their heads. Patches covered eyes, and stained slings cradled broken arms. And the less obvious wounds could be seen deep within each airman's eyes—the depression and sense of hopelessness. Not long ago, these men had been healthy and vibrant airmen fighting against a threat to world freedom. They had fought with hope and lived each day out knowing that someday they'd return home to their families. They had now become a formation of tattered and tired, hungry and sick, demoralized and wounded prisoners who were being treated like a herd of cattle. For all they knew, their lives could end in this rural region of northern Germany.

Marching alongside the columned prisoners were armed German soldiers, their rifles a deadly deterrent to any escape attempts. The group marched through the center of town down a cobblestone road lined with two- and three-story buildings. Puddles from an earlier rain had accumulated in pockets of missing stones in the tortoiseshell road. Inside a third-story hotel window, an elderly lady peeked down at the prisoners as they marched through the town. A few onlookers cracked their wooden doors to look at them.

Daniel looked into a street-level window decorated with white shutters. Inside, loaves of dark rye bread sat in wicker baskets. The smells of fresh baked goods that escaped from the drafty door tormented the prisoner's appetite. Never before had a dense loaf of bread looked more appetizing to him. He was reminded of his father's grocery stores—small, personable and welcoming. LaHurd's glimpse of his own reflection in the bakery window lurched him back to the present. Overgrown whiskers formed a stubbly shadow on his cheeks, neck and chin. His thick hair and full mustache were greasy, matted and filled with dirt.

As the group of worn prisoners departed the village, LaHurd looked back upon it. He knew this was the last time he'd see something other than his prison camp until the end of the war or the event of his death. A light mist, almost a fog, covered the grassy fields just outside the village. The steeple of a Lutheran church, half veiled through the low-lying gray clouds, marked the aged city. The group marched north for two hours until they came to the gates of their new home, all expenses paid by the Führer.

Through the trees, a guard tower stood tall, overlooking an expanse of dirt and mud. Large shaved tree trunks supported a wooden box where a guard stood peering out of open windows. Another guard walked down the narrow zigzagged staircase. Power lines drooped into the structure, most likely the energy source for the large spotlight that hung from an outside corner. The first line of fencing that the prisoners came to encircled the entire camp. Just beyond the two large wooden doors of the first gate sat administration buildings and what seemed to be a hospital. Beyond that were acres and acres of wire fencing, erected logs stripped of their bark, wooden and brick structures and a sea of dirt and rust. Just outside the confines of the camp sat a large flak school and an airstrip. There were no churches, no grass, no civilians and no appealing smells here. Daniel had never seen anything so dreary in his life.

The first step before registering and processing the prisoners was to mitigate the potential spread of disease. The men were stripped of their clothing and placed in a large open room, where they were deloused and given their first shower in weeks. As the men enjoyed their three-minute wash, their clothing was placed into boiling vats of water, the intense heat killing any clinging bacteria. They were also given the option of a fresh shave. LaHurd enthusiastically accepted the razorblade. He was careful to stay clear of his now sweeping mustache. The prisoners finished their showers and dressed in their damp clothes. Each man was photographed by an impatient administration worker who wore the swastika on his shoulder with immense pride. His brow furrowed as he looked each prisoner over with disgust. He fingerprinted LaHurd and placed a new metal tag around the prisoner's neck. The tarnished rectangular metal sheet stamped with "Stalag Luft 1 4852" now hung next to Daniel's other two oval dog tags that recorded his name, serial number, tetanus immunization and toxoid, blood type and religion. To the Nazis, LaHurd was no more than a number in their growing list of prisoners.

After the registration process, the POWs received their new bedding and eating utensils. LaHurd's pile of goods contained a dilapidated burlap mattress filled with wood shavings, a towel, two thin army blankets, a cup, a bowl, a knife, a fork and a spoon, all engraved with the swastika.

LaHurd and the other initiated prisoners were soon ushered through a number of gates guarded by Nazis and dogs. Fencing dissected the larger camp into different compounds. On the opposite side of the fences, caged within their cordoned cities, veteran prisoners lined the wire, hollering out names as the new group was escorted into their determined compounds. *Stalag Luft I* was separated into four of these compounds: West, North I, North II and North III. Each compound consisted of about nine to fourteen barracks.

Daniel looked around at a gang of unfamiliar faces screaming and shouting through the wire, "Hey, hey, more *kriegies*.* How long until these goons crack and surrender?"†

---

* The English translation of *kriegie*, short for *kriegsgefangener*, is prisoner of war.
† The POWs called the German guards goons.

"Welcome to the Hitler Hotel," yelled another *kriegie*.

Another prisoner called out, "I sure feel like a heel, forgot to get you swell boys a housewarming gift!"

Over the prisoners' jibes, Daniel heard, "Danny Boy!!"

To his right along the fence stood Smitty squeezed in the crowd.

"Goddamn, I knew you'd be all right," said Smitty.

His stay at Dulag Luft had been three days shorter than LaHurd's. The two men had never known they were in the same interrogation camp at the same time. Solitary confinement kept any prisoner there oblivious to any happenings outside his own cell.

Aside from the joy of seeing a familiar face, LaHurd was fortunate that he had been recognized so quickly. Frequently, new prisoners were shunned and ignored until someone could claim them as an Allied soldier. Thankfully, Smitty was there to identify his bombardier. Otherwise, the men behind barbed wire would have had no way of knowing whether the unknown prisoner was a German spy in disguise.

LaHurd was marched into the North II Compound carrying his new possessions. He looked around and counted nine dilapidated barracks within the eleven-acre compound. Small gardens just outside each barracks grew root vegetables. A structure serving as the kitchen and another doubling as a chapel and theater accompanied the living quarters. The cooler—a six-cell brick building used for solitary confinement—also occupied land in the compound. Prisoners found themselves inside the cooler when they were caught trying to escape. The *kriegies* could also find themselves in the cooler for insubordinate remarks to German guards, failure to salute German officers of equal or greater rank, destruction of compound property and other minor acts of disobedience.

LaHurd had been assigned to Barracks Three, Room Five. Each of the wooden barracks had ten to thirteen rooms partitioned off inside. The long unit stretched 50 feet by 150 feet. To Daniel, the shabby barracks resembled a covered bridge, long and narrow. His new shelter housed over 150 men. That number slowly increased over the course of the war as more and more airmen became POWs.

He entered his new home just as a gust of wind blew over the parade ground, kicking up the dusty earth. Inside, a long hallway stretched to the opposite wall, where another entryway was located. The corridor was dark and forbidding. LaHurd's room was on the west side of the barracks, at the opposite end of the latrine in the northeast corner. Just outside to the east, another ominous guard tower stood. The Nazi inside was ready to shoot anyone who came within four feet of the fence, otherwise known as no-man's land. A metal wire designated this forbidden strip of space. If a prisoner so much as put a limb over the line, he was gunned down.

LaHurd entered his room escorted by a guard and another *kriegie*. The room was colorless, messy and dank. Laundry hung to dry from ropes that crisscrossed the ceiling. Footlockers stood next to the wooden framed bunks where men's personal belongings were stored. The small room slept twelve officers. Two dirty blankets and a stained pillowcase sat on each bed of the double-stacked bunks. The bedding was washed only once a month. Occupants' poems, artwork, maps and letters hung on the wooden walls. A cast-iron stove, a wooden table with a pair of benches and loose items such as cards, journals, mugs and clothing filled the interior. LaHurd was shown his new bunk, where he laid out his flat mattress and eating utensils. In the corner, a brick chimney rose up through the roof. The stove's exhaust made from connected klim* cans hooked into the brick vent. The room was humid and held a sour odor. Daniel knew he'd have to get used to these things.

He was quickly briefed by the barrack's commander, Captain Jay Jaynes. The gist of the briefing: "Don't try and escape alone because you'll get killed. If you have any ideas on how to escape come to the escape committee and work out a strategic plan." LaHurd was informed of the command structure and taught the acronyms and nicknames used around camp.

After his briefing, Daniel had the remainder of the day, the remainder of the week, the remainder of the month and God only knew how long after that to find his place at the camp. For the most part, the *Luftwaffe* complied with the laws of the Geneva Convention, which stated that captured officers did not have to participate in work detail. Without work and without a reason to train, the prisoners had to pass time as best they could.

He met a few of his new roommates who were lounging around the room. An officer from the Eighth Air Force handed Daniel a few pieces of bread with a frugal amount of spread. He gratefully accepted the much-needed calories.

It had been another long and exhausting day, and Daniel was worn out beyond comprehension. The stubborn sun hung at the horizon until nearly midnight. The prisoners were locked in their barracks, the window's shutters closed and locked and the lights ordered off at 11:00 p.m. The only source of fresh air was a small ventilator. LaHurd lay back and closed his eyes in this foreign, uncomfortable place. How long would he be here? He

---

* Klim, or milk spelled backward, was dried milk.

Photograph of Daniel LaHurd taken at *Stalag Luft I* during registration.

was grateful that he was surrounded by other American officers and that his interrogations and solitary confinement were over, but he was worried about how long his stay at *Stalag Luft I* would last. What if his wife slowly forgot about him or the Allies won the war and left him here to die? Even worse, what if there was a turn of events and Hitler's Germany won the war? He brushed his mustache with his fingers and pushed the thought from his mind.

A couple of lamps, recycled tin cans filled with margarine for fuel, burned throughout the room, their flickering flames flashing *kriegie* shadows across the walls. Outside, an eerie silence swept over the camp. Occasionally, an Alsatian's bark or a shriek pierced the silence.

"Nice to have ya here, Danny. Sleep tight, and we'll see if we can find your buddy Smitty tomorrow," whispered one of Daniel's roommates.

LaHurd had met all of his roommates throughout the evening. Each man had quickly accepted Daniel, and before long, the guys were joking and sharing stories.

LaHurd's last thoughts before closing his eyes were of his wife, Calvin and Ryan. He also dreamed of his mother's home-cooked meals. His starving stomach gurgled for her food. He lay there reminiscing about his mother standing in the kitchen on so many Sundays preparing a large feast.

Tomorrow, he'd search for Smitty and other members of his group. But presently, he needed rest.

Chapter 14

LOST BOYS

August 8, 1944–September 1, 1944

They have given their sons to the military services. They have stoked the furnaces and hurried the factory wheels. They have made the planes and welded the tanks, riveted the ships and rolled the shells.
—*President Franklin Roosevelt, on women's contribution to the war*

On August 8, 1944, after a long day of work, Madeline LaHurd left Goodyear AirDock to catch a streetcar. Exhausted, she dragged her low-heeled shoes across the ground to the car's stop three blocks away. Her blond hair was pulled back, kept out of her face by a tightly knotted blue bandanna. The late afternoon humidity caused her slack suit to stick to her body.

She looked down at her hands. Her fingers had become cracked and callused from her difficult job as a riveter. The aircraft she helped to manufacture could potentially be the fighter that would someday guide her husband home. One of those fighters could someday save Daniel's life. That was her fuel to keep going. Like many American women, she saw the equipment she built as an integral part in the fight to stop tyranny, defend freedom and ultimately protect the men of her country. Everyone had a husband, brother or father serving overseas, or if not that, at least a neighbor or friend.

Madeline boarded the streetcar that would take her a block from Mary and Pa Joe's home. She had made dinner arrangements with the LaHurds. The family tried to stick together as much as possible during these tough times. Their company seemed to ease one another's fears and hold depressing thoughts about Daniel and Calvin at bay.

The trolley was crowded with women of all ages—teenagers still in school, teenage dropouts earning income for their families, middle-aged ladies and women over fifty. Their duties in the workforce ranged from riveters to spot and torch welders, hydraulic press operators to crane operators, inspectors to office help. Madeline made her way through the crowd to the rear of the car. Drained of energy, her legs struggled to keep her body balanced as the streetcar accelerated forward. She tightly gripped a steel bar that hung overhead. She knew she would have to stand for the majority of the ride. A young woman reading a newspaper sat in a seat next to where Madeline stood. Headlines covered the usual news of battles, victories, list of known deaths, war bond advertisements and endless predictions of Hitler's surrender. Fighting the stubborn wrinkled paper and packed aisles, the young woman struggled to turn the page as Madeline looked down to catch a glimpse of the front page. Just off to the side of the bold headlines "Yanks Race Towards Paris," she saw a disheartening picture of a burning B-17. Squeezing her way between a few passengers, Madeline politely asked the lady if she could take a closer look at the front page.

The sun outside the car's windows began to approach the horizon. The light inside the car was dim, but the black-and-white picture was clear. She checked for names under the article's headline, "Air Battle Rages Over Europe." As she read, she prayed that Daniel's name wasn't listed in bold font. The thought of him never returning from combat made her heart sink. But the crew of this bomber in the paper was a member of the Mighty Eighth. Her husband was safe for now.

The streetcar slowly decelerated to Madeline's stop. It was not uncommon for these working women to exit the streetcars and factories with tears in their eyes from exhaustion, depression and anxiety. Madeline dabbed at her tears with a small white handkerchief as the streetcar driver gently wished her a good evening. She bashfully nodded in response.

On the street, Madeline collected herself and straightened her shoulders. She removed her bandanna and picked at her hair with her fingertips to give it some fullness as she made her way to the LaHurds' home. Children played baseball on empty roads, the fielders and batter of the game occasionally disbanding to make way for an automobile. Older folks watered their gardens, now fully ripe from the hot summer sun. The government encouraged these Victory Gardens, since the shortage of harvesters and transportation made it difficult for farmers to garner and move fresh produce. Many farmers had been drafted, and trains were needed to transport war material instead of fresh vegetables and fruits.

The darkening August sky was filled with a gray storm cloud off to the west. The distant cloud rose high into the atmosphere, a flattop marking its highest point. Faint rumbles of thunder rolled across the evening air.

Approaching the LaHurds' home, Madeline could see Mary and Pa Joe sitting on their front porch steps. Joseph held Mary in his arms. Mary's face was softly illuminated by the evening light. Pa Joe's face was partially obscured by an oak tree's shadow swaying in the breeze.

As Madeline came closer to the porch, she heard a soft whimper coming from Mary. For a moment, Pa Joe just stared blankly at Madeline. Then he gently released his wife, rose and took his daughter-in-law's hand. A group of clouds leisurely moved in from the west. The headlights of a Ford pickup truck flickered down the street as it drove over the brick road running in front of the LaHurd residence. The humming of the rubber tires against the uneven brick progressively grew louder and then softened as the truck passed. Children's arguments over whether the pitcher threw a strike or ball echoed through the neighborhood as their game came to an end.

Pa Joe's stoic face looked the same as always, but the trembling, weeping body of Mary was proof that something had gone terribly wrong.

Pa Joe hugged Madeline and whispered the news he had received from the Fifteenth Army Air Force just hours ago. "Daniel," he paused, trying to gather the words for what he had to say. "Daniel's plane was shot down over Germany, sweetheart. The plane went down almost three weeks ago." He seemed unsure of what to say next. "We can only pray that he made it out okay and that he is on his way to safety. I'm sorry, sweetheart. I'm truly sorry."

Thunder grew louder. Leaves from the tree-lined road tumbled through the sky and settled wherever the wind decided to drop them. Rain would soon be pouring down from the dark, saturated clouds directly overhead.

Madeline's knees turned to jelly. She and Pa Joe, the wife and father of the missing airman, knelt together on the sidewalk, wept and prayed.

FIFTEENTH AIR FORCE
Office of the Commanding General
A.P.O. 520

8 August, 1944

Mrs. Mary LaHurd
1099 Berwin Street
Akron, Ohio

My dear Mrs. LaHurd:

I am extremely sorry that I must confirm the notification you have received from the War Department informing you that your son, First Lieutenant Daniel E. LaHurd, 0-741271, has been missing in action since July 18, 1944, when his Flying Fortress failed to return from a daylight bombing mission over Memmingen Aerodrome, Germany.

Dan's plane was severely damaged by enemy fighters and as a result is believed to have gone down in the general vicinity of the target. Because of the demands of aerial battle accurate observation was impossible and we therefore are unable to report whether any parachutes were used. Until official word is received on the status of the men we can do little but wait and hope for the best.

You can be sure that the War Department will notify you as soon as more detailed information is available.

For wounds received in action and for meritorious achievements throughout sustained combat operations Dan has been awarded the Purple Heart and the Air Medal with two Oak Leaf Clusters. You can well be proud of his record and the service he has given his country in her hour of need.

Very sincerely yours,
N.F. TWINING
Major General, USA
Commanding

Joe and Mary assisted Madeline into the house from the sidewalk. Madeline felt her hopes of building a future with her husband shatter. The chances that he had been killed were high, injured even greater.

The evening's meal sat cold in the center of the dinner table. The LaHurds' desire for food had evaporated when the letter's contents were unveiled. Mary provided Madeline with a fresh change of clothes and suggested that she stay the night. Joe informed the rest of the family of the terrible news. The family collectively decided to keep the information of Daniel from Calvin. The two brothers were very close, and the family didn't want the news of Daniel to lower Calvin's morale.

The thunderstorm eventually unleashed its fury over the neighborhood. Lightning flashed through the night sky like a strobe light. Thunder roared. Gusts of wind blew rain down in thick sheets. After a barely eaten dinner, Pa Joe, Mary and Madeline sat quietly in the living room. Pa Joe, legs crossed and a small Bible resting on his lap, stared out the window as raindrops tapped at the glass. He could not help but sit inside his home and compare the noises of thunder and the flashes of light to exploding bombs and cannon fire. Each clap outside caused him to jump as he thought about his boys overseas.

Mary sat, rosary hanging from her interlocked hands, and whispered prayers for her two sons' safety, her head tilted slightly to one side. The last time she had seen Daniel and Calvin was on their furlough home over a year ago. Would she ever see them again? She wondered if her Daniel had been killed.

Like her mother-in-law, Madeline sat motionless and stared into space. Jumbled thoughts ran through her head—Daniel's current whereabouts, past memories of them together, questions about their future. She couldn't help but picture the worst-case scenario: her husband alive but experiencing excruciating torture by the Nazis. She feared that he was being boiled in hot oil or skinned alive. Her eyes had been drained of tears; they were bloodshot and heavy now. She looked down at a basket of letters, each penned and sent by Daniel or Calvin to their parents. Pa Joe and Mary had accumulated the mass of letters over the past two years. So many days had been taken from this family by this war. Important past events captured by ink rather than actual experiences together. Madeline yearned to create these memories with Daniel in the flesh. She yearned to see her husband.

Joe looked at his wife. He knew there was nothing he could say to assuage her fears. He himself wanted to believe that Daniel was alive. He wanted to believe even more that Daniel had found safe refuge, but the endless stream of stories written across the pages of the newspaper over the years brought doubt to his hopes. The local *Beacon Journal* had recently written:

FOUR MORE SOLDIERS FROM AKRON DISTRICT KILLED IN ACTION

Two parents in a little Springfield twp. home re-read a V-mail letter with teardimmed eyes Tuesday.

"Dear Mom—Keep praying. I'll do my best and as much as I can to win this war."

It was the last letter P.F.C. Gerald Stump, 21, sent home to Mr. and Mrs. Ellis Stump before he died on the last day of July on a battlefield in France. The letter was dated July 28, and the soldier said he was writing it in a foxhole.

He was one of two Akron district men reported killed in the drive through France. In addition, two men missing in action for a year, now are declared killed in action.

Returned mail began to find its way back to Akron soon after the family heard news of Daniel's status. This was the mail that had never reached Daniel at Sterparone Airfield. To make matters worse, Pa Joe received another letter in the mail only a week later, August 15, stating that Private Calvin LaHurd was missing in action. Two sons lost in Europe. The family had found it difficult enough to deal with one son missing, but now two sons were gone.

On August 22, after an emotionally torturous two weeks, confirmation came from the government that Daniel was a prisoner of war. Jubilation filled the city of Akron and the house at 1099 Berwin. Daniel was alive. To the LaHurds, alive in a prison camp was better than lying dead in Germany. There was still hope that they'd see Daniel again.

Aug. 22, 1944
Government, Washington D.C.

Joseph M. LaHurd
Report just received through the international Red Cross stated that your son First Lieutenant Daniel E. LaHurd is a prisoner of War of German Government. Letter of information follow from Provost Marshall General.

Madeline wept grateful tears. Her husband was alive. It was at this moment that she knew he would return home. She felt it deep down inside her.

The next day, the headline story read:

Brightest news of the day was the word that one of the two missing LaHurd brothers, Lieutenant Daniel, has been reported as a prisoner of war of the Germans....Another LaHurd brother, Pvt. Calvin C., a soldier in France, is still listed among the missing. To Joseph LaHurd, secretary of the Grocers Institute, Inc., and his wife, the news that one of their sons is alive in a prison camp came as a reprieve from constant worry over two sons lost within a week of each other.

Only weeks after receiving official word that Daniel was a prisoner of war, Mary received an unusual anonymous letter. The return address read France. The *Akron Beacon Journal* reported on the contents of this splendid letter. The headline of the article: "Lost Akronite Safe, French Letter Says":

"Madame LaHurd" received a letter from the heart of France the other day.

Never before had the wife of Joseph LaHurd, secretary treasurer of the Grocer's Institute, Inc., had a missive addressed to her in just that fashion.

But the Frenchman who wrote it had taken no chances on his letter to "Madame" being lost in the long journey overseas. Plainly, for the censors to read, he had inscribed on one corner of the envelope the words, "important letter with good news of a prisoner from America."

...Written partly in very poor English and partly in French, it told the overjoyed mother that her second son, Private Calvin LaHurd, 20, is still living....

"You excuse me, I write you in French, because I write not very well English," he said.

"I give you some good news of your son. I have seen him in this little village the last week. He had good health. The Germans took him at St. Lo."

The writer, having exhausted his English vocabulary then turned to French.

"The Americans passed yesterday, which was Sunday, in this small village where I am a refugee from Caen. Your son came last Wednesday with his detachment as a prisoner of war of Germany. But I assure you he is in good health and well treated. All day yesterday he and I spoke English. We were happy and I was happy to have such a wonderful friend. I made him promise to write to me always."

Joseph and Mary didn't receive official word that Calvin was a prisoner of war until late November. Four tortuous months of worry and despair passed before the army sent a letter officially stating that he was a POW. The LaHurds' worry was somewhat eased knowing that at least both of their boys were alive. All they could do was pray for them and hope for the best.

Chapter 15

MONOTONY

August 1, 1944–March 31, 1945

And I looked, and behold a pale horse: and his name that sat on him was Death,
and Hell followed with him.
—*Revelations 6:8*

Daniel LaHurd slept surprisingly well through his first night at *Stalag Luft I*.
As a matter of fact, it was the best sleep he would have during his tenure at
the camp. Twelve men living in Room Five limited the space. The crammed
quarter's air was thick and humid in the summer and cold and bone-chilling
in the winter. His mattress consisted of fabric stuffed with woodchips. Adding
to the discomfort were the atrocious screams that frequently echoed through
the night air. Somewhere within the stalag, airmen awoke in cold sweats as
they relived their terrifying missions deep in their dreams. The whimpers
and shrieks were enough to drive a man mad.

Daniel eventually located his pilot and navigator. Smitty was assigned to
the adjacent compound, and Stein was just a couple of barracks away. They
had both bailed from the B-17 on July 18 with only a few minor scratches
and bruises. Over time, Daniel would slowly attain information on the other
crew members of *Virgil's Virgins*.

During his first week at the camp, he had been marched off to the
hospital, still within the outer fences, where the taciturn doctors disinfected
his cuts and put a clean set of bandages on him. His chest injuries healed,
and the deep bruising slowly vanished. As the days advanced and the warm
temperatures slowly turned cold, the men of Barracks Three, Room Five,

began to bond. All the men really had at the stalag were countless empty hours spent with one another. Every new day that passed wasn't much different from the previous one. Guards patrolled the fences and stood alert in the towers, prisoners were counted twice daily, minor cleaning duties were carried out, athletics were played when the weather permitted and each man made do with his rationed food and three-minute-long frigid weekly shower.

The rumors that had floated around Sterparone about prison life were accurate. They were long days absent of any occupation. The voids in time were filled with repeated conversation. The prisoners told childhood stories, described their wives and girlfriends and made promises to one another of lifelong friendship. But sincerity and companionship weren't always the norm around *Stalag Luft I*. Closely corralled boys in their late teens and early twenties brought about conflict as well. Proximity and personality clashes, in addition to underlying feelings of depression and anxiety, caused many to argue and even physically fight. Fortunately, Daniel and the others of Room Five didn't have such a problem.

More than the Nazis, time had become the prisoners' worst enemy. One could only listen to his roommate's childhood stories so many times, or read for so many hours, or play cards without cash for so many hands. The common substitute for dollars at the stalag became cigarettes. Instead of winning a pot of cash at poker, the prisoners preserved their interest by betting with cigarettes. These sticks of rolled tobacco became the economic backbone within *Stalag Luft I*. Fifty smokes could be traded for a candy bar or five thousand for a wristwatch. And although restricted by *kriegie* law, these prized cigarettes were traded with the Nazi guards for valuable commodities.

The days behind the wire were the longest days of LaHurd's life. Each was filled with an abyss of nothingness. A man had little reason to set goals in such a confined space. Daniel spent his afternoons, weather permitting, walking laps around the compound. This was his way of keeping his mind and body strong. He had made a promise to himself to stay in shape mentally and physically under any circumstances. He swore that he wouldn't let the stalag change him like he had seen it change others, that he wouldn't lose his personality and charm. He knew that once he lost that, the goons had won the battle.

The uncertainty for the prisoners proved to be even worse than the boredom. What were the prisoners' wives and girlfriends doing back home? How long was this war going to go on? Would the prisoners ever see home again? There were very few answers to be found. The hopeless and

WRITE VERY CLEARLY WITHIN THE LINES. IN ORDER TO EXPEDITE
CENSORSHIP, LETTERS SHOULD BE TYPED OR PRINTED IN BLOCK CAPITALS.

Dear Dan;

        We got your address yesterday and that made us happy
beyond what words can express. I got busy on the telephone
and spread the good news to all of the family, starting with
Mel and down the line to our close friends. You were reported to us as missing on August 8th and on August 22 we were
notified that you were a prisoner of war and of course have
been praying that we would soon hear from you. All of us
have been brave and held up very well under the strain and
was surprised that your Mother held up as well as she did.
I went to the Red Cross

depressing days led many prisoners to simply clam up and become mutes. There was even a diagnosis for this condition: "Barbed Wire Syndrome."

Daniel hated the fact that he was here, but there was nothing he could do about it. He knew that his wife and family back home were scared to death about his well-being. The thought upset him very much. He couldn't do anything but write and tell them that he was okay. Letters home were limited each month to four three- by five-inch cards and three five- by twenty-inch letters. Every penned sentence was read by German censorship. If the Nazis weren't satisfied with the letter's contents, the words were blocked out with thick black marker or the letter was simply thrown away.

Every day, LaHurd awaited a letter from home. Sometimes they came, but more often they didn't. His family was writing daily, but nowhere in the long list of German priorities was timely delivery of *kriegie* mail listed. When mail did come, LaHurd's morale was lifted tremendously. The letters sent from home had never before been so appreciated and desired.

September
Akron, Ohio

Dear Dan;
We got your address yesterday and that made us happy beyond what words can express. I got busy on the telephone and spread the good news to all of the family, starting with Mel and down the line to our close friends.

You were reported to us as missing on August 8th and on August 22 we were notified that you were a prisoner of war and of course have been praying that we would soon hear from you. All of us have been brave and held up very well under the strain and was surprised that your Mother held up as well as she did. I went to the Red Cross... [This section censored and blacked out with marker] *...Fred and Maryellen are still honeymooning and have paid off the debt on their furniture and have started to put a little money in the bank each week. Mike and Boo-Boo are getting along just as nice as ever and Neil is going to be a big man as he has sprouted out in the past year. And Linda Lou is a little chatter box talking all the time and a couple years ago we were afraid she would not learn to talk. Loads of love and kisses from all of us to you.*

Mother + Dad

October 31, 1944
Starlag Luft I

Dear Folks
Here's hoping this finds you all in good health—me—well!—I'm swell and getting along fine—so please don't worry. Ya can send some playing cards—ours are about gone—Getting to be a fair bridge player—Can also send some—cigars—candy—spices—package soup—Thanks—Ya some wool sox + scarf.

Love
Dan

Nov. 14, 1944
Akron, Ohio

Dear Dan;
[This section censored and blacked out with marker] *...We are sure your well. Always felt that the Germans treated prisoners as well as they could under war conditions. Calvin is well as the rest of the family. Mary-Ellen and Fred are 3 months with a child and will be parents in May....Hope you received the 6 cartons of cigarettes and package I sent you last month. We go to church every Sunday and pray that you and Cal will come home safe and sound. The Red Cross advised to limit our letters to 8*

each month, so we agreed to have Mel write once a week and once a month
for Mike, Fred, Lou and myself. Don't worry about us as we are well and
hope to stay that way as long as you and Cal are well. Loads of love from
each and every one of us.

Mother and Dad

As a captured private, Calvin was sure to be living a more grueling and arduous prison life than his officer brother. The LaHurds in Akron were receiving even fewer letters from Calvin than they were from Daniel. The family had made a difficult decision to keep the news of Daniel's capture from Calvin and Calvin's capture from Daniel. They didn't want to add any more stress to their boys' already stressful situation.

Throughout autumn, LaHurd and his roommates became obsessed with the Allied offensive. Each mile the Allies drove closer to Berlin meant the prisoners' liberation and ultimately the conclusion of the war was that much closer to becoming a reality. Who would the liberators be? Would it be the Russians from the east or the Americans and Brits from the west? An entire clandestine operation within the stalag was occupied with pumping out war information every night. The newspaper bulletin *POW WOW*, or *Prisoners Of War Waiting On Winning*, was passed out to the prisoners. The content of the paper came from a hidden radio that was able to transmit British Broadcasting Company news. The other source of information was through the new arrivals, as each new prisoner brought with him current information on the war and the Allies' progress.

Each of LaHurd's days started the same, with roll call on the parade ground at 8:00 a.m. The prisoners were counted off one by one. If the count was off, there was a recount, and all absent and valid medical lists were checked. If someone was still missing, each person was identified and called by name. Roll call was never skipped or taken lightly. Rain, snow or shine, the prisoners were out on the parade ground twice a day. The longer the count took, the longer the men had to endure the elements of nature. The same exercise took place again at 4:30 p.m., just before the men were locked in their barracks. By 11:00 p.m., the single dim bulb within their room was shut off.

The single most important part of the prisoners' day was food. Food took precedence over warmth, cleanliness, entertainment and even sleep. The Nazis stingily provided the prisoners with bread, potatoes, rutabagas, kohlrabi (turnips), salt, ersatz* coffee, jam, sugar and cheese. The dense, dry and moldy bread was the same tasteless bread that Daniel had eaten in interrogation. He was convinced that he burned more energy trying to swallow the dry crumbs than he gained from eating it. The oily jam provided little flavor. The potatoes were soggy and moldy, and Daniel promised himself that after liberation he would never eat a rutabaga again.

The saving grace for the *kriegies* was the American Red Cross. These lifesavers shipped food parcels from Switzerland when available at the rate of one per man per week. They contained the following items: spam, corned beef or C-ration stew, salmon or sardines, pate (meat paste), jam, klim, powdered coffee, oleo (margarine), cheese, half-pound box of sugar, raisins or prunes, crackers, two field ration D-bars or one can cocoa, five packs of cigarettes and one box of vitamin pills. The barracks gardens also produced some root vegetables, though that source of food vanished when the arctic temperatures came.

The most welcome source of food came from personal parcels sent from family members back home. Each prisoner was allowed one box every two months, and the nonperishable items inside were well worth the wait. LaHurd's packages were always filled with *kriegie* delicacies—nuts, hard candy, cigarettes, cake mix, fruitful jams, chocolate and delicious canned foods. Pa Joe knew how to fill every square inch of the box with wonderful items. These personal parcels were shared among the men in the room. Roommates anxiously gathered around each time a personal package was delivered, their stomachs ready to lurch out of their skin and attack the rare cargo. Mouths salivated at the thought of what was inside. The *kriegies* of Room Five knew they were lucky. They loved when LaHurd's personal parcels came, since they knew that his father ran grocery stores. Pa Joe had the ability to obtain foods that most families back home didn't have access to.

Just as the Nazis censored *kriegie* mail, they spent an equal amount of time searching *kriegie* parcels. Any pepper or strong spices were confiscated. Prisoners could use these items to throw in the eyes of guards and dogs during escape. Every canned food item was punctured, severely limiting the edibility of the meats and creams inside to only a few days. This eliminated the *kriegies* from building up a cache of food or packing it away for a long escape. Because food was the most important part of a prisoner's life, the Germans knew that if they controlled the food, then they controlled the prisoners.

---

* *Ersatz* is a German word literally meaning substitute or replacement.

On the homefront, the LaHurds were among a group of thousands that had a family member in a prison camp somewhere in the world. Every day, the stalags in Europe and prison camps in Asia were growing in population. Madeline, Mary and Joseph started every morning with a long prayer asking God to protect Daniel and Calvin. Many families of Calvin's unit and Daniel's crew whispered the same prayer each day.

By late autumn, the families of Daniel's crew had begun collecting information about their son's or husband's last mission over Memmingen. They had obtained the names of the other crew members on that fateful day and began to seek out answers to their many questions. Letters from the stalags to home were slow, sporadic and received months after they had been written, so the parents and wives of *Virgil's Virgins* started their own research.

Nov 7, 1944
Huron, So Dak.

Mr. Joseph M. LaHurd

Dear Mr. LaHurd,
We received a list of names from the war department of the air crew members that were in the same crew as our son, as your son was listed as one of them. I am interested to know if you have had much information from him, as we have only had two cards from our boy which were written July 25 and Aug 1st stating he was well and a german prisoner and that he would write later, but, we have had no word since. We would be very grateful to hear from you if you have had any news or information from your son or any of the crew members as their familys where they are I will send you our sons address so you can compare it with your sons. We write often but do not know if the letters get thru.

Sincerely
Mrs Anna Venables
Sgt. Lloyd V. Venables,
United States prisoner of war #7013
Stalag Luft 4
Germany

Nov 25, 1944

Mr. Joseph M. LaHurd,
Through the War Dept. I have been informed that your son 1ˢᵗ Lt. Daniel E LaHurd was a member of the crew of a flying fortress on July 18, 1944 when the plane was lost.

My son was also a member of the crew Sgt Horace A Davenport, I am trying to find out if any of the crew was saved. I have been informed that my son was killed. I have seen one boy that was in another plane but he did not know the fates of the crew that my son was with.

I would like very much to know if your son was taken prisoner or not. If some of them could just be captured possibly sometime we could find out more. Any information you could give me will be highly appreciated.

From Mrs Annie E Davenport and husband
Pelzer, SC
Route No 2.

———

November 29, 1944

Mrs. Anna E. Davenport
Route Number Two
Pelzer, South Carolina

Dear Mrs. Davenport:
Our hearts are bleeding for you at the loss of your son as we can appreciate how you must feel in this terrible tragedy that has come to you.

We were very fortunate that Daniel was able to parachute safely. He is a prisoner in Stalag Luft No. 1 which is in Barth, Germany. He wrote a postal card on July 24ᵗʰ and a letter on August 1ˢᵗ, which we received on October 30ᵗʰ saying he was in good health and well treated.

My other son Calvin was reported missing in action at St. Lo, France on July 27ᵗʰ, nine days after Daniel was reported missing and we did not receive official word until Monday of this week that he is a prisoner.

We received word that Sgt. Carl E. May and Sgt. John E. Papamonoli are prisoners but to date we have not heard from the families of the other crew members.

We will write to you if we receive any information concerning your son.

With deepest sympathy, we are
Very truly yours,
J.M. LaHurd

———

175

Nov-26-44

Mr. J.M. LaHurd
1099 Berwin St.
Akron, Ohio

Dear Mr. LaHurd
I have information from the Army Air Force Headquaters that your son 1ˢᵗ
Lt. Daniel was aboard a flying fort with my son S/Sgt. John on July 18
when they were shot down over Memingen, Germany.
*   My son is a prisoner in Stalag Luft No. 4. and I hope your son was saved.*
*   Will you please let me know if you have any news from Daniel and if*
he mentioned anything about my son. The only news I had from my son so
far was a card written on last July 24 where he said that he was a prisoner
and received good treatment. Ever since I have written him several times but
cannot get any letter from him.
*   Hoping to hear from you*

yours truly
E.J. Papermanoli
308 Tyler St.

───

11-27-44

Mr. Joseph M. LaHurd
Dear Sir,
Through the Gov I have been informed that your son was a member of a
crew of a flying fortress that was lost on July 18ᵗʰ 44. Was your son taken
prisoner by the Germans or did he lose his life? Our son S/Sgt. Carl E
May is a prisoner of War in Germany + we have been wondering since
how many of his crew was still living, we have one card from our son + it
was written July 24ᵗʰ 44 + we didn't receive it until Sept 26, He said he
had landed in Germany + was taken a prisoner + was in good health +
was being treated well + praised the red cross for their kindness. We have
hoped and prayed for the safety of all the crew with our son, but we received
a letter from a Mrs. Davenport from S.C. stating that her son had been
killed. We hope that your son landed safely + with our son + we will all
be reunited before to long. A letter from you at any time will be appreciated.
yours very truly,
Mr + Mrs. Charles E. May
Hymesa, Indiana

As the winter months crept by, the camp became frozen tundra. Snow constantly blew in a sideways direction as wind swept over the open ground. A deep layer of powdered snow replaced the dust and dirt. Trails of icy slush filled *kriegie* footprints that crisscrossed throughout the parade grounds leading from one barracks to another. The men were spending most of their time cooped up inside their quarters. The outdoor temperatures were just too cold. The moment roll call ended, the *kriegies* rushed back inside their rooms, where rationings of coal burned in the stove, providing some warmth.

LaHurd spent the freezing days writing in his journal while shivering under a thin blanket. He copied down poems and songs. One of his favorites was titled "Hitch in Hell":

> *I'm sitting here thinking of things I've left behind*
> *But it's hard to put on paper what's running thru your mind*
> *I've flown lots of missions over lots of foreign ground*
> *A drearier place this side of hell is still waiting to be found*
> *But there's one consolation sit closer while I tell—*
> *When I die I'll go to heaven for I've done my Hitch in Hell*
> *The angels all will meet me and harps will start to play*
> *Then I'll get that greeting reserved for that special day*
> *It's then I'll hear St. Peter say loudly with a yell*
> *Take a front seat brother you've done your Hitch in Hell*

By Christmas, journals and playing cards had been pushed aside. The *kriegies* prepared for the holiday. Some prisoners made Christmas ornaments; others spent time decorating the walls with scraps of paper they painted with watercolors that had been donated by the Red Cross. The *kriegies* built a camp Christmas tree with a broom handle and strips of wire cut from klim cans and decorated it with toilet paper cut and colored to simulate needled foliage. Cigarette packages became tinsel. Soap wrappers, tin can labels, notebook covers and slivers of paper became artificial snow. Much to the *kriegies'* appreciation and surprise, the Nazi guards pushed back curfew on Christmas Eve and allowed the prisoners to attend a midnight Mass. That night, the usual screams and cries that pierced the night air were replaced with baritone voices singing Christmas carols.

Daniel's family continued to communicate with him through the holidays. He would only receive sporadic letters, but he knew that his family had him in their prayers and hearts during the Christmas of 1944. His first Christmas as a husband was spent behind barbed wire. His dear Madeline would have to wait for the war to be over, and he prayed that he would spend next Christmas cuddled up next to her under a warm blanket.

6 December 1944

Dear Dan;

Yesterday we received word that Calvin is well and sound and has been in Germany since 27 July. I wrote to him that you are in good health and being well treated and mentioned you spoke over the radio on 27 October. Fred moved to our house last week, his wife is working at the Credit Bureau but will quit soon, as she will be a mother by Easter. Mel is working steady and is as beautiful as ever. Mike is still with Lever Co. and Beulah is 3 months gone, so you will be an Uncle to 2 more next year. Neil has got to be a big boy this year and Linda is a darling. Al and Lou are doing well and Mary Lou is as sassy as ever and Allyn is a husky boy and will make as good a football player as his dad. Last but not least Ma is as pretty and young looking as ever. As for me, I am grateful and happy that you and Cal are alive and with the rest of the family am looking forward to the day you and Cal come home. Loads of love and kisses.

Mother + Dad

———

December 8, 1944

[This section censored and blacked out with marker]...*As soon as we receive mailing labels from the War Department we will send you 2 packages of tobacco and 1 of food....Mel is feeling good and looks as sweet as ever. Is working everyday and seems to like her work. Lou and Al are as busy as ever, Al in the store and Lou watching over the children. The love birds...*[This section censored and blacked out with marker]

———

Dec. 27, 1944
Akron, Ohio

Dear Dan;

Just wrote to Cal who is well. Christmas was quiet for everyone. Beulah took communion on Xmas and I gave her a Rosary + Prayer Book. Ma got a nice dress for Mel and Mel gave Ma a pocket book and gloves for me. Hope you have received the Cigs, and packages we sent you. Let me know what to send you when I can....This town has not changed one bit, the same routine....We are very proud of you and pray that the good Lord will watch over you and keep you from harm. All of us are well and hope this finds you in the best of health. Loads of love + Kisses

Mother + Dad

Through the holidays, Pa Joe continued to write letters not only to Daniel and Calvin but also to the families of the captured crew members of *Virgil's Virgins*. If and when Madeline had free time, she spent it writing to her husband, so Pa Joe told Madeline that he'd write to the crew members' families. By mid-December, the survivors of *Virgil's Virgins* had been at their stalags for nearly five months. Their families never gave up hope and continued to search for more information on their captured sons and husbands.

Dec. 4, 1944
916 Bedford Ave.
Collingdale, Pa.

Dear Mr. LaHurd,
I received your letter and was very glad to hear Danny is safe also. My husband is a prisoner in Stalag Luft No. 1. He wrote a post card on July 26th which is all I have received from him. However he spoke over a short station on September the 26th. I didn't hear him but the War Department sent me the message saying he was in good health and treated well and a few other things. All the prisoner's have the privilege of speaking over the radio and if you haven't yet been notified Danny was heard, you have a very good chance of hearing him. The program comes on two nights a week from eight P.M. to ten P.M.

I have heard from six of the men's mothers and fathers, all are prisoner's but one that I know of Sgt. Davenport was reported killed.

I'm so very happy that you also had good news of your other son Calvin. It must have been a great strain on you. Thank you for your interest in my husband and thank you for writing. I appreciate it very much.

Sincerely,
Mrs. M.J. Smith

Dec. 11th 1944
Putneyville, Pa.

Dear Mr. LaHurd:

Was very pleased to receive your letter. Thank you for writing.

Was glad to hear your son is safe. We assume he was the pilot of the plane. Are we right?

Our son is also a prisoner at Stalag Luft No. 4. The Red Cross tells us that camp is near Stettin, Germany. We received a card from our son written on July 23rd, and on last Friday Dec. 8th we received a letter written on Aug. 11th in which he said he was well, and not to worry.

Until we received your letter we did not know if they made a forced landing or used parachutes. However, if your son used a parachute then the rest must have done likewise.

We have heard from seven of the crew through the parents, so far one boy reported killed, and one hospitalized. We know just how happy you must have been to hear your other son is alive too. Being a prisoner isn't pleasant yet we do have hopes of their return some day when this mess is all over.

Sunday, Dec. 10th was our prisoner son's birthday, was 21 years old, and one birthday he will always remember. Do you know the name of the plane of which your son was a member of the crew?

Our son was not an original member of crew that went on the July 18th mission. The pilot of their ship, as well as four other members of the crew were at a rest camp so our son and four other members of his crew were sent in the plane in which your son was a member. This information we learned from the pilot of our son's plane and through his parents at McKeesfort Pa. Our son sent us a list of the names and States from which they came, of the members of their crew before he went overseas 1st of march. The July 18th mission was our son's 39th mission.

We have a son 19 yrs. of age on the aircraft carrier U.S.S. Enterprise and has been in the thick of the Philippines battle, in Halseys 3rd Fleet.

May God Bless and keep our sons safe is our fervent prayer, and that they may all return to us some day. Hope you hear from your son Calvin soon, and that he is well too.

Most Sincerely
Mr. + Mrs. W.S. Doverspike

December 29, 1944

Mrs. Rebecca Stein
101 South Third St.
North Wales, Pa.

Dear Mrs. Stein:
Very glad that David is alive although a prisoner and pray that his leg
injury is not serious. Sorry to hear about your son Jack and hope you'll hear
from him soon.
We didn't have official word that Calvin was a prisoner until December
4th which was nearly four months after we were notified on August 14th that
he was missing in action on July 27th.
We received a postal card, two letters and a short wave message from
Dan but his clothes haven't come yet. No doubt you have also heard from
the families of the other crew members but to make sure I'll repeat that
eight boys are in prison camps, Marlin in a German hospital for critically
wounded and Davenport was killed.
I join with you that the boys will be home early in 1945.

Sincerely,
J.M. LaHurd

By February 1945, Germany's economic instability, the failing Nazi regime, winter and revenge for the firebombing of Dresden made *kriegie* life increasingly more difficult. Hitler demanded that the Reich kill all prisoners of war in retaliation for Dresden. The order was never carried out. Field Marshal Hermann Göring convinced Hitler that the Allies would surely retaliate against that act of murder by killing German prisoners. The *kriegies'* lives were spared, but life became even harder. The Germans essentially stopped feeding the POWs and cut off all Red Cross parcels. Food became scarce behind barbed wire, limited to rotten potatoes, stray cats, gluey barley soup with insects and slices of the awful bread. The average human body needed nine hundred to one thousand calories a day to survive healthily. During February, March and April, the prisoners at *Stalag Luft I* were given one bowl of watery soup and two slices of bread daily.

LaHurd wrote in his journal, "I don't know if we will be able to go another 3 or 4 months like this. We may be in some real big trouble." The depleting feline population caused the rat population to grow. Throughout the barracks, the infested rodents roamed freely. Outside, the temperatures

Thousands of *kriegies* line up for morning roll call outside their stilted barracks.

Sporadic groups of *kriegies* battle the cold temperatures inside the barbed wire of *Stalag Luft I.*

The inside of a barrack room at *Stalag Luft I.* Resources and food are scarce. Nothing goes to waste.

were below zero. Water troughs and plumbing were frozen. Showers became nonexistent.

Every new day brought with it more and more prisoners. German camps in Poland were being evacuated into camps deeper within Germany as the Russian front pushed west. The barracks' rooms became crowded, and food became even scarcer. Double-stacked bunks were transformed into triple-stacked bunks. The unwashed prisoners and overflowed latrines released an incomprehensible smell.

Other than leaving their barracks for roll call, the prisoners spent the majority of their day shivering in their bunks, trying to keep warm and doing their best to conserve energy. It was one of the harshest winters in German history. Each day became an act of survival. Lacking fuel, the stoves inside the rooms burned only occasionally, and when they were lit, the welcoming heat was brief. Liberation couldn't come fast enough. The men inside the camp were slowly dying.

Chapter 16

LUCKY

April 1, 1945–June 17, 1945

*This is a solemn but glorious hour. General Eisenhower informs me that the forces
of Germany have surrendered to the United Nations. The flags of freedom fly
all over Europe. For this victory, we join in offering our thanks to the Providence
which has guided and sustained us through the dark days of adversity. Our
rejoicing is sobered and subdued by a supreme consciousness of the terrible price
we have paid to rid the world of Hitler and his evil band. Let us not forget, my
fellow Americans, the sorrow and the heartache which today abide in the homes
of so many of our neighbors—neighbors whose most priceless possession has been
rendered as a sacrifice to redeem our liberty.*
—President Harry S. Truman

Just as things really started to get unbearably tough at *Stalag Luft I*, the
weather began to lift and real food was offered again. The Nazis were
retreating back into Germany and were more concerned with defending
Berlin than starving the POWs. Furthermore, the guards knew the war was
lost for them, and the Allies would soon seek reparation for maltreatment.
Consequently, a few days before Easter, food came into the camp by the
truck load. Instead of trying to starve the prisoners, the guards helped to
feed them. One could call it insurance after defeat. An attempt to cultivate
companionship with the new occupiers of Germany couldn't hurt.

The temperatures outside slowly began to rise, the snow and ice began
to melt and in between the heavy rains, the *kriegies* were able to venture
outside again for some much-needed fresh air. With the food came

backlogged mail. Daniel received a letter from his sister, and it gave him a new-found hope. It was an instantaneous morale booster:

February 5, 1945

Dearest Dan,

Today was your first wedding anniversary so Pa, Ma, and I went over to see Mel and we all drank a toast that you would be together on your second. What a difference a year makes! It seems only yesterday that you two were married.... We got a letter from Cal dated Oct. 23ʳᵈ and he wrote one to Fred Nov 12ᵗʰ. He sure sounds good and assures us not to worry about him. He hasn't had any mail from us since the first of May so I bet the poor kid is plenty anxious about us. He says he prays for you every night because he doesn't know you're a prisoner. Alan will be 2 years old Feb. 27ᵗʰ and he is a right husky ladapple of his grandpa's eye.... Fred + Maryellen are getting along fine and their baby is due next month. Can you imagine Fred a father? Please let us know as soon as you hear from any of us as we do want you to know we are all fine and please don't worry about us. Mel is fine too + is pining away for you. Love and kisses from everyone of us Dan.

Bye for now—Lou.

As the days of April pressed on, the prisoners grew more impatient for their liberation with each passing day. The hidden radio confirmed what the *kriegies* were hearing and seeing from outside their barrack's windows. At night, bombs could be heard exploding in the distance. During the day, dogfights and attacks over the airfields just outside Barth could be seen. Overhead, rumbles from groups of Allied bombers moved across the sky deep into Germany, where they unloaded their bombs. The Allies had crossed the Rhine, and the Red Army was only weeks, if not days, away from crossing the Oder River. The *kriegies* could hardly bear the suspense. Would the Nazis allow them to be liberated or would they murder them instead? Would the airmen be liberated by the Americans or by the unpredictable Russians?

On April 30, Daniel awoke to screams coming from the parade ground. His thinned body, weighing 125 pounds, torpidly rose out of bed to see what had caused the commotion. Each day through the end of April, the sounds of artillery grew louder and stronger in the distance. It was an audible ballet, suspenseful and mysterious, from somewhere in the east. The intensification of explosions proved to the *kriegies* that the Russians were on the offensive and they had started their push across the Oder River. Though the exploding shells were still miles away, the blasts were strong enough to rattle bunks and shake the earth under the stalag. Not only did the distant explosions test the structural integrity of the ceiling rafters, but they also stirred the emotions and morale of the confined men within.

Daniel made his way out of the barracks door, squinting from the sunlight, to see *kriegies* hugging one another. The screams were not of horror but of jubilation. The Germans had fled, and the camp's Nazi flag had been replaced with a handmade American flag. The Stars and Stripes had never looked more beautiful to him in all his life. The Germans were gone, and the swastika flew no more.

Only hours earlier, the Nazi commander of the prison camp had met with Colonel Zemke. The American colonel was an intelligent man, a strong leader. He had prepared for an array of outcomes at the stalag—liberation, forced death march, SS or Gestapo slaughters and Russian occupation. The best-case scenario was an Allied liberation from the west, but the bombs from the Red Army to the east had proved this to be unrealistic.

The conversation between the two leaders had been brief but stern. The Nazi guards who manned the towers could be more accurately compared to civilian farmers than soldiers. The original, authentically military guards had been displaced weeks earlier from their towers to the diminished front lines to defend their homeland. As the Nazi commander of *Stalag Luft I* finished covering his planned march of all prisoners from the Baltic camp to camps deeper into Germany's interior and away from the pressing Russian front, Zemke had retorted that his men would not march; they would stay put and fight if they had to. The colonel expressed his confidence that the ten thousand airmen under his command armed with makeshift weapons could crush the two hundred greenhorn guards. Zemke promised a massive and mad rush of every tower. In the end, the ploy worked. The Nazi commander was supplanted by Zemke. The Germans fled from potential Russian capture not long after the meeting.

Freedom. At first, the idea of it was impossible for LaHurd to register. Not a day had gone by in his approximately nine months of captivity when he hadn't thought of freedom. He looked around in disbelief. If all went well, he would be home in a matter of months, maybe weeks, to look his beautiful Madeline in the eyes before pressing his lips to hers. The thought of his wife's warm touch sent excitement through his body.

After a few seconds of standing in place like a stunned deer in headlights, he ran out into the yard, grabbed the nearest prisoner's shoulders and screamed, "Those kraut bastards are gone!" He laughed aloud. "Can you believe it, those kraut bastards are gone! We're going home!"

The guard towers were now occupied by Americans, yet the gates were still locked and the fences still intact. The war was not yet over, and the *kriegies* had to contain their urge to stampede from the camp out into a dangerous country filled with pockets of Nazi soldiers. The airmen within the towers, under order from Zemke, were to watch for intrusive action but also enforce that the *kriegies* remain within the camp's gates. Although difficult to accept, it was entirely possible that at any hour a rogue SS division could sweep through the camp and slaughter the ten thousand men. Only a few days earlier, Adolf Hitler had ordered that all prisoners in the stalags be shot, one of the Führer's last-ditch efforts of insanity and murder. The threat of death within this shattered country was still very real.

Not long after the departure of the Germans, the hidden radio picking up the BBC crackled the news of Hitler's death. More cheers of jubilation filled the Baltic air. The culprit who had started this entire European mess was finally dead by suicide. The men began to excitedly tell stories to one another of their future plans, hopes and dreams. The thought of home, American soil, fresh food and independence was just over the horizon.

The next day, a Russian officer, who later would turn out to be an enlisted imposter, rode through the gates of *Stalag Luft I* on horseback demanding that the prisoners be released. With much hesitation, Zemke, believing that the Russian was of higher rank than he actually was and eager to avoid a clash with Allied Russia, complied. LaHurd and his roommates, along with the rest of the men in the camp, tore down the gates and fences and spread throughout the countryside. The exodus of free men looked like a herd of cattle running across an open plain. LaHurd scampered to Barth with a number of his fellow prisoners. The town quickly became inundated with ex-*kriegies*.

Daniel made his way to the large church. The image of its steeple cutting through the gray clouds in late July 1944 had been burned into his mind. It had been the last piece of architecture he saw as a free man. He entered the massive wooden doors and sat in the front pew for hours thinking of home. His heart thumped in his chest from excitement. If all went right, he would be home soon.

Before heading back to the camp, he stopped in at the bakery for a fresh loaf of bread. He hadn't stopped thinking about the smell from his initial encounter when he had marched through the city nearly nine months ago.

While the Russians began to set up camp to protect the prisoners and occupy the area, Russian General Borisov noticed the lack of healthy and hearty food. He had live cattle, cows and pigs sent in for the airmen to eat. LaHurd helped butcher the fresh meat, carving out fatless filets and strip steaks for the prisoners. Complimented on his skills, he thought fondly of his father and the grocery store that had provided the training for this moment.

LaHurd contemplated fleeing for the west every additional day that the men were kept corralled by Zemke and the Russians. Bureaucracy would delay evacuation of *Stalag Luft I* for days and days. The land surrounding Barth was officially under Russian control, and logistics needed to be worked out among the Allies. LaHurd and a small group of Americans could wait no longer for the politicians to figure things out. They finally chose to head for the west on their own. Daniel and three others commandeered a tattered German vehicle and headed down unknown roads leading in the direction of the setting sun. Their first few days were spent driving over the bumpy roads of western Germany. As the men bounced across the country, they were astonished by the vast destruction. Cities and towns were leveled. Concrete was pulverized into pebbles. Glass windows were nearly nonexistent. Craters and devastated forests covered the countryside.

The four officers spent their first night in Wismar and made their way to Luneberg the following day. It was in a Luneberg restaurant that they heard the extraordinary news over a crackling radio. A friendly and hospitable local acted as the group's waiter and translator. The Germans had surrendered at Berlin, and the war in Europe was over. The group celebrated with pints of thick frothy beer. From Luneberg, the men headed for Brussels, where they ditched the car, stayed the night and hitched a ride on a cargo train that took them to Paris. By May 12, just as LaHurd and the other three men hopped from the train in Paris, the Russians and Americans had finally agreed upon and implemented Operation Revival to extract the remaining prisoners at *Stalag Luft I*. For two days, the prisoners were marched to the airfield just outside the camp. Groups of B-17s landed there in short intervals, picking up thirty men at a time and evacuating them to the safety of the west. Daniel's route from Barth to France was indisputably more dangerous than waiting for the extraction, but he didn't care; he hadn't wanted to stay behind barbed wire any longer. He wanted to be a free man, and he wanted to get home.

LaHurd and his cohorts spent a fabulous day and night in Paris. The hours were filled with alcohol, dancing and eating. The city was a big party, and the heroes were the American boys. After the twenty-four-hour festival in the City of Light, LaHurd made his way to Camp Lucky Strike, an

Allied embarkation camp. The camp, just one of many bearing the name of American cigarettes, was located inland just outside the city of Le Havre in the town of Saint-Sylvan, France. It resembled a city with its twelve-thousand-plus pyramidal tents that stretched as far as the eye could see. The men coming into the camp were the most ragtag and worn-down-looking group to ever coalesce in Europe. These soldiers had just won a war, and their stinking bodies and dirty, tattered clothing proved it.

LaHurd, now classified as a RAMP (returned Allied military personnel), showered in warm water without a time constraint for the first time in nearly ten months. Standing there with the water splashing in his face, he knew what his next action would be. He had to find his brother. The chances that Calvin was at Camp Lucky Strike were slim. News of his brother over the past months had been scarce. Daniel had little idea where Calvin was, but he needed to look for him.

After showering, he was deloused with DDT powder spray, given new clothing, served a hot meal and assigned to a tent. That night, he welcomed the comfort of his American-made cot and slept soundly. The following day, he was debriefed and given a physical examination. Then he began the search for his younger brother. The mass of troops and sea of tents made his task seem impossible, but after a week, his luck and determination finally paid off. He wrote home to his parents, informing them that Lucky wasn't only the name of the camp but something much more:

May 21, 1945
France

My Dear Folks
How are ya all? I bet ya feel a 100% better now that this damn war is over and us boys, meaning Cal + I of course, will be home soon. I would have wrote much sooner but I thought I'd leave Lucky Strike Camp much sooner—fact is I thought I would only spend a couple of days here—I ought to quit thinking seeing as how I spent nine days here already and it looks like I might spend another nine days before I'm processed. All we've done here so far is eat which is a good habit but I'd much rather get home to Ma's cooking and maybe take a chance at one of Mel's meals. Hell! I can't keep the surprise any longer so here goes—Hold your seats yah! your to sharp for me—ya guessed it. I ran into that handsome six footer of a kid brother of mine and he sure looks swell. I hardly believed my eyes but there he was reading notices at the Red Cross—that ended my week search for him and it was well rewarded—looks to me like he put on weight but I

wouldn't know seeing as that's the first time in almost two years I've seen the brute. Pronto he was moved from his area to my tent which I share with two buddy officer friends of mine. Cal now is living uptown—from a fourteen man tent to a four manner. His old area was about a mile from mine but now we'll go home together so get the kibbeh ready.

Say hello to everyone for me and we'll be seeing you all soon.

Love
Dan

The two brothers spent the next few days exchanging war stories and informed each other of their prison camp experiences. Calvin's overcrowded stalag had been liberated only a day before Daniel's by General Patton's Third Army. The boys were amazed that their parents had been able to keep their status as prisoners from each other. They both agreed it would have made things more difficult if they had known. The two traveled to Paris together, which was only a two-hour journey from the camp. Their trip lasted a week, drinking the best wine and eating the best food.

But there was still no place better than home. The delay to return stateside was frustrating. Soldiers were arriving by the thousands on a daily basis to the embarkation camp, which created a huge backlog for processing and shipping. The daily influx of men created a three- to four-week delay in availability of ships to transport the soldiers home.

June 4, 1945
France

Howdy! Folks

I sure bet you've been sweating out our return but so have we. I guess it won't be long now as we're getting to be some of the few thousand XPOW's left out of something like 90,000.

Cal and I are both well but anxious as all hell to get home on that sixty day leave—we'll sure have a big time—just think the whole family together again for sixty days—Yipee!! Hey! Mike or Fred haven't been caught in the net yet—have they? Hope not. How are ya all? How many times am I an uncle? There's a million questions I want to ask so I best save them till I get home.

Bye now with loads of love to you all—don't forget to kiss Ma for me and get that Kibbeh ready.

Love
Dan

June 4, 1945
France

Dear Folks,

Dan and I are still in the old country, done with all the processing just waiting for the boat to take us home and to you. So far, all we've been hearing are promises and no definite action. We're both getting darn disgusted. I hope and General Eisenhower told us we should be home by the end of this month. So let's just wait anxiously together for this long month to end.

To pass the tiresome days, we've been eating, sleeping and going to various shows. So far the weather is lousy but otherwise the both of us ex P.O.W. are okay. Our health is superb so no need to worry. I hope everyone back home is alright. God Bless and keep you safe and healthy.

Love Cal.

Eventually, the brothers' patience paid off. By June 17, the two men were on a boat steaming toward the United States.

Chapter 17

BOMBARDIER'S PROMISE

June 17, 1945–July 23, 1945

Humility must always be the portion of any man who receives acclaim earned in blood of his followers and sacrifices of his friends.
—*General Dwight Eisenhower*

The Atlantic Ocean's vast expanse buoyantly supported a massive transport ship forged from steel. Displaced water splashed away from the ship's bow, intermittently drowning out the noise of the roaring engines that propelled it from France to America. The stretch of salt water served as a mirror to the afternoon sun situated directly overhead, reflecting the daylight from the greenish ocean back into the sky. The seas were not unusually rough. The waves were just high enough to produce a repetitive rocking motion sure to make any non-sailor seasick for the entire three-day journey home. Seasickness was inevitable for Daniel's sensitive stomach, but standing on the outside deck at least eliminated the claustrophobia from the tight confines of the lower decks where Calvin was napping.

Daniel stood portside looking out at the distant horizon with a slight grin across his face. He could almost taste his mother's home cooking and feel his wife's touch. His arms crossed, he leaned against the railing that bordered the ship's deck. The sun beat down on his head. The wind blew against his face. The misty spray of the Atlantic cooled his skin. This bombardier was finally on his way home where he could hug and kiss his wife, on his way home where he could see his family and friends. He had been granted a sixty-day pass that he could spend with his wife and family. He could meet his new sister-in-law, see his new niece and nephew, spend time with his brothers and love his new wife. After that, he didn't care what happened. He guessed that he'd probably be shipped off to the Pacific to fight the Japanese.

His boat arrived at Camp Patrick Henry, Virginia. There waiting for him and Calvin were his cousin Walt and Daniel's good buddy Tony Testa. While the group planned their voyage home by train, Daniel told them that he had one last mission to complete before heading back to Akron. He wanted to see his wife and family badly, but it would have to wait just a little bit longer.

Daniel walked up to the stoop of an attached apartment building in the Bronx. An American flag hung from the door's side. The bombardier sucked in a deep breath of New York air, adjusted the nametag on the right breast of his uniform and centered his cap.

A nameplate over the porch light read "The Ryans." A small bead of sweat began to form just below his hairline as he made his way up the three steps leading to the front door. His breathing grew heavy. His heart began to beat faster, and he noticed the thumping in his chest. His mouth became dry. He tried to control his emotions.

The woman who opened the door was not much different in age than his own mother. She looked at the soldier who wore a similar uniform to that of her son. As the airman removed his cap, the woman began to recognize his face from photographs that had been sent home by her son. Photos filled with images of the two men laughing together, playing poker together, saluting each other, smoking cigars together, studying together, eating together, training together, living together and traveling the world together. She looked down at the man's nametag to confirm her recognition: "LaHurd."

She slowly stepped onto the porch. At first, no words were exchanged. Mrs. Ryan had been informed nearly a year ago that her son was killed in action. She was proud that her boy had given his life defending the United States, but she struggled to come to grips with his death. The mother of Arthur Ryan grabbed Daniel's shoulders and pulled him close, and the two hugged as the tears flowed. All the two could do was hug and cry.

After wiping her tears away, Mrs. Ryan led Daniel into her living room. Behind the couch, he noticed a console table decorated with pictures of his friend. Daniel sat. To his right, resting on an end table, was Arthur Ryan's framed officer's picture. Situated on the top of an oak mantel was a tightly tucked triangular American flag. He broke the silence by explaining to Arthur's mother that the two men had made a pact in Italy. The pact had ensured the brothers-in-arms that their names would live on if one man was killed in action. Ryan had promised that if Daniel perished, he'd name his firstborn son Daniel Elias Ryan. Daniel had promised that if Arthur perished, he'd name his firstborn son Arthur Ryan LaHurd.

Daniel had come to the Bronx to inform Mrs. Ryan that her son's name would live on. He told her how brave and admirable her son had been. Mrs. Ryan was speechless, only able to cry and smile. Looking at her, Daniel gave a silent prayer of thanks, praising God that his own mother didn't have to go through this experience.

After a short visit, Daniel was finally ready to travel home. The two promised each other that they'd stay in contact. With that, Daniel departed.

Chapter 18

VICTORY GARDEN

July 24, 1945

Victory at all costs, victory in spite of all terror, victory however long and hard the road may be; for without victory, there is no survival.
—*Prime Minister Winston Churchill*

Mary and Madeline knelt in the grass, diligently working to rid the side yard garden at 1099 Berwin of weeds. Smells of mint tickled their noses. Bright red tomatoes and fresh peppers hung from the perfectly aligned plants in paralleled rows. Various raised mounds of dark, rich soil ran the length of the garden, punctuated by a trellis at the far end. Grapevines crawled up from the ground and across the interwoven oak frame. Thick foliage of tender leaves and grapes grew in abundance there.

Three days earlier, Calvin had walked through the door to a mother weeping from joy and a father succumbing to his pent-up emotions. Mary and Pa Joe had greeted their son with what seemed like an endless group hug. Calvin had smiled at his parents' warmth and love and the sights and smells of home. The foxholes, cold and prison camp fences were gone.

Mary hummed quiet melodies and Madeline fantasized about her husband's return as they meticulously pulled rooted invaders from the dirt. A small wicker basket sat on the ground, holding freshly picked vegetables that would soon fall victim to the kitchen knife. Madeline could hardly wait any longer to be with Daniel, to hug him, kiss him and simply look at him. She pictured her husband walking into the house, winking at her and the two running to each other with open arms. From the year 1944 to the spring of 1945, Madeline had watched the clock tick away day after day as she waited for the war to end. But the past few months had seemed even longer. She knew the war was over. She knew Daniel was free. She just wanted him back. Why was it taking so long for him to come home?

Suddenly blocking the summer sun, a long dark shadow interrupted her thoughts.

"How have my two ladies been?" asked a tender voice.

Madeline and Mary turned in unison to see Daniel standing over them with a tear in his eye.

He was finally home.

Chapter 19

ONE LIFE

Americans in uniform served bravely, fought fiercely and kept their honor, even under the worst of conditions. Yet they were not warriors by nature. All they wanted was to finish the job and make it home.... These were the modest sons of a peaceful country, and millions of us are very proud to call them "Dad." They gave the best years of their lives to the greatest mission their country ever accepted. They faced the most extreme danger, which took some and spared others for reasons only known to God. And wherever they advanced or touched ground, they are remembered for their goodness and their decency.
—President George W. Bush at the World War II
Memorial Dedication Ceremony

Without question, the greatest war the world has ever encountered ended less than a century ago. From the brutal armies of ancient Greece to the current war on terrorism, the world has never been as fully engaged in war as it was from 1939 to the fall of 1945. Cities around the world were reduced to rubble, and the loss of life was incomparable to any other act of man that written history can account for. At its conclusion, fifty-seven million civilian and military lives from more than sixty countries around the world were lost. Countless other individuals were physically or mentally incapacitated due to this cataclysmic event.

At the beginning of World War II, the United States had a small and somewhat weak military. It ranked sixteenth in the size of its armed forces. In 1939, the United States military was made up of only 334,473 personnel, a small number in comparison to the 12,123,455 men who called themselves American soldiers in 1945. Almost 300,000 of these U.S. soldiers perished during the war.

In 1939, just before the Second World War began, 13 B-17s existed. Six years later, at war's end, over 12,700 of these machines had been manufactured at a cost of $276,000 apiece, equaling nearly $3.2 million today. In the early 1940s, a new car sold for $1,100, a new home cost around $8,000 and minimum wage was thirty cents an hour. The average American's yearly income was $2,500. So the staggering $3.5 billion spent on the Fortresses through the course of the war proved their importance.

From its inception to V-E Day, just under a year and a half, the Fifteenth Air Force, originally consisting of 3,544 B-24s and 1,407 B-17s, lost 1,756 B-24s and 624 B-17s. Of the original crew members in the 483rd Bombardment Group sent to Italy, a staggering 39.8 percent were either killed in action or declared missing in action.

All of these statistics are made up of individuals, each possessing a unique story of death, love, fear, victory and defeat. One of those individuals, my grandfather, logged twenty-six hostile missions, 168 combat hours and 663 hours of total flight time over the skies of Europe. Each minute spent in the air was a stressful and equally fear-filled experience always unique to the mission at hand. His years of training and studying never could have prepared him for the sights, sounds and smells of what proved to be the most transforming experience of his life.

Each mission may have finally rested on the shoulders of the ten trained crew members inside each bomber, but it also traced back to people at home, from engineers to factory workers to farmers and housewives. Those civilians' frugality, hard work and patriotism all played a quintessential role in each infantryman, seaman and airman's success, ultimately leading to a victory for the Allies.

Daniel LaHurd never had to fight over the skies of the Pacific. The Japanese surrender in August 1945 brought an end to his combat experience. By November 1945, Daniel's military service had concluded, and he was finally able to start the life that he had dreamed about while overseas stuck behind barbed wire fencing at *Stalag Luft I*.

As the anxieties of the Second World War slowly dwindled and the newspapers turned to other events, Daniel and Madeline began to build their lives together close to their family in Akron, Ohio. Arthur Ryan LaHurd was born on April 16, 1946. Daniel and Madeline had three more boys: my father Dennis and twins Douglas and Daniel.

When my grandfather was eighty years old, he was interviewed by a local Sarasota news channel regarding the Serbian captivity of three American soldiers during the crisis in Kosovo. As he sat on his favorite recliner, he answered the interviewer's questions with utter heartfelt sorrow for the three prisoners. I could see right past his healthy Florida tan into his deep brown eyes to the sadness and the return of tender memories. At my grandfather's home overlooking a pond in his backyard, the reporter asked him if he had any words of advice for the captives.

"I feel bad for them. They need to be brave." He paused a moment, lost in thought. "Just be brave and everything will turn out okay for them, I hope."

Throughout the Second World War, millions of American soldiers and over ninety thousand American POWs, coupled with an entire civilian nation, had to be brave in the face of their uncertain futures and a powerful fascist enemy. Undoubtedly, those years of world chaos and upheaval changed an entire generation and their outlook on life. But bravery, as my grandfather asked the three prisoners in Kosovo to seize, led to a victorious outcome for the United States.

Daniel LaHurd lived the rest of his life to the fullest. He lived for the moment. His days in the bombardier pod had exposed him to life's fragility. His moment of hurling to the ground in a burning B-17 had helped him appreciate his existence. The months behind barbed wire had made him realize that life was what one made of it and freedom could easily be stripped away. These military experiences may have explained my grandfather's spendthrift lifestyle and go-with-the-flow attitude. He always lived for the now. He had faced death a number of times. He had faced tremendous odds against his life, not just once, but twenty-six times. He knew that he was lucky to be alive and took full advantage of living.

I asked my father, "How did the war change Grandpa?"

My father chuckled and answered, "I don't know. He never talked about it. He was always known to be happy and carefree, helpful and giving, fun and comedic. Even a war couldn't change those things about him." My father paused, thought for a moment and added, "But I think his war experiences made him take chances more in life. He never hesitated to take risks, open a business or spend money. He knew the important things in life: honor, respect, kindness and family."

Daniel LaHurd's love for gambling, business, family and golf only grew with age. I often wonder what kind of man my grandfather would have been without those four life-altering years of world war, those years when he had limited contact with his family, built friendships that were stripped away by combat and knew that he must have killed unknown numbers of people by the touch of his thumb. But that war and those experiences ultimately shaped the man whom I knew as my grandfather; the man whom the LaHurd family knew as dad, brother, uncle, husband and son; and the man whom many others knew as a friend.

The next time you pick up the newspaper or a history book to read about war, I hope you can see past the large statistics. These multi-digit numbers take so much away from those meaningful words: honor, respect, kindness and family. Many people say that the Second World War was fought by the greatest generation in our nation's history. I believe this war was fought by the greatest individuals in our nation's history. Let us never forget the sacrifices that these courageous individuals and their families made in the name of freedom.

WRITER'S NOTE

The primary goal for this book was to accurately inform readers of my grandfather's actual experiences during World War II. However, some pieces of the story were modified by me to strengthen the entertainment factor.

A few specific items: The scarred *unteroffizier* from chapter 1 was created by me. My grandfather talked about a Nazi soldier riding up to him on a bicycle just as he hit the German soil after bailing out of his bomber. The activities and appearance of that German soldier on the morning of July 18, 1944, are fictitious.

The actual holding place of my grandfather in Kempten before going to Dulag Luft is unknown. Therefore, the barn, the interrogations (although research did show that many of the prisoners taken to Kempten faced a low-level interrogator) and the meeting with Papamanoli were my renditions. The reason I chose Papamanoli was to tell the actual events of Davenport's death and Marlin's injuries. Due to Papamonali's position on the aircraft, he was an eyewitness to Davenport's and Marlin's statuses.

Although Calvin LaHurd was captured during Operation Cobra and "The Dash" just outside St. Lô, the events of chapter 12 are my creation, along with the names read off at the prison camp.

BIBLIOGRAPHY

Akron Beacon Journal. "Lost Akronite Safe, French Letter Says." August 1944.

Ambrose, S.E. *The Victors.* New York: Touchstone, 1998.

———. *The Wild Blue.* New York: Simon & Schuster, 2001.

Army Air Forces. *B-17 Pilot Training Manual.* Army Air Forces, n.d.

The Aviation History On-Line Museum. "Messerschmitt Bf 110–Germany." 2006. Retrieved August 28, 2008. www.aviationhistory.com/messerschmitt/bf110.html.

Bossie, C. "Deming Army Air Field." Desert Wings. July 14, 2005. Retrieved August 28, 2008. www.angelfire.com/dc/jinxx1/DAAF/DAAF.htm.

Bradley, J. *Flyboys.* New York: Back Bay Books, 2003.

California State Military Department. "Santa Ana Army Air Base." April 20, 2008. Retrieved August 28, 2008. www.militarymuseum.org/SantaAnaAAB.html.

crispcreation@sbcglobal.net. "The Story of the Memmingen Mission." Bombardment Group (H) Association. 2000–07. Retrieved October 7, 2007. www.483rd.com/index.html.

Crosby, H.H. *A Wing and a Prayer.* New York City: Harper Paperbacks, 1993.

Davisson, B. "Analyzing the Ryan Recruit." Airbum. 2003. Retrieved August 28, 2008. www.airbum.com/pireps/PirepPT-22.html.

Delcamp, M. "War Stories." Interview with C. LaHurd, September 13, 2008.

Douhet, G. *Command of the Air.* Translated by D. Ferrari. New York: Coward-McCann, 1942.

Farmer, A. *Teach Yourself the Second World War*. Chicago: Contemporary Books, 2004.

Field, T.A. *The Shack: Class 43-5*. Deming, NM: Aviation Cadets of Deming Army Air Field, 1943.

Freer, M.S. "The Roomates." 2008. *Stalag Luft I* Online. Retrieved December 29, 2008. www.merkki.com/north2.htm.

Friedman, T.L. *From Beirut to Jerusalem*. New York: Anchor Books Paperback, 1990.

Global Aircraft Organization. "B-17 Flying Fortress." 2000–08. Retrieved August 28, 2008. www.globalaircraft.org/planes/b-17_flying_fortress.pl.

Grimm, J.L. *Heroes of the 483rd*. N.p.: 483rd Bombardment Group Association, 1997.

Hicks, M. "War Stories." Interview with C. LaHurd, September 13, 2008.

Hofbauer, M. "Panzerfaust." August 29, 2001. Retrieved September 2, 2008. www.geocities.com/Augusta/8172/panzerfaust3.htm.

LaHurd, C. "Operation Cobra." Interview with C. LaHurd, September 12, 2006.

LaHurd, D.E. "War Stories." Interview with C. LaHurd, August 24, 2001.

LaHurd, M. "Rosie the Riveter." Interview with C. LaHurd, January 18, 2008.

Lingeman, R. *Don't You Know There's a War On?* 2nd ed. New York City: Thunder's Mouth Press/Nations Books, 2003.

Miller, D.L. *Masters of the Air*. New York: Simon & Schuster Paperbacks, 2006.

Ochoa, R.E. "Hondo Army Air Field." The Handbook of Texas Online. January 19, 2008. Retrieved August 29, 2008. www.tshaonline.org/handbook/online/articles/HH/qch2.html.

Official Museum of the United States Air Force. "Beech AT-11 Kansan." Retrieved August 28, 2008. www.nationalmuseum.af.mil/factsheets/factsheet.asp?id=484.

———. "Focke-Wulf Fw 190D-9." Retrieved August 28, 2008. www.nationalmuseum.af.mil/factsheets/factsheet.asp?id=507.

———. "Messerschmitt Bf 109G-10." Retrieved August 28, 2008. www.nationalmuseum.af.mil/factsheets/factsheet.asp?id=505.

———. "Ryan PT-22 Recruit." Retrieved August 28, 2008. www.nationalmuseum.af.mil/factsheets/factsheet.asp?id=479.

OhioStatebuckeyes.com. "Football: 1942 National Championship Team to Be Recognized at Halftime of Northwestern Game." September 21, 2007. Retrieved August 27, 2008. www.ohiostatebuckeyes.com/ViewArticle.dbml?DB_OEM_ID=17300&ATC LID=1245699.

Richard, O.G. *Kriegie*. Baton Rouge: Louisiana State University Press, 2000.

Rickey, S. "War Stories." Interview with C. LaHurd, September 13, 2008.

Sebby, D.M. "Visalia Army Air Field." California State Military Museum. May 18, 2008. Retrieved August 28, 2008. www.military museum.org/VisaliaAAF.html.

Smith, J.W. *The Propwash (Class of 43A Sequoia Field)*. Visalia, CA: Aviation Cadets at Sequoia Field, 1942.

TIME. "Trouble in Akron." August 1944. Retrieved August 27, 2008. www.time.com/time/magazine/0,9171,932732,00.html?promoid=googlep.

Vietor, J.A. *Time Out*. New York: Aero Publishers, Inc., 1951.

Waterhouse, H. "Four More Soldiers from Akron District Killed in Action." *Akron Beacon Journal*, August 23, 1944, 11.

Westheimer, D. *Von Ryan's Express*. Garden City, NY: Double Day & Company, Inc., 1964.

Witkowski, T.H. "World War II Poster Campaigns." *Journal of Advertising* 32, no. 1 (2003): 69–82.

WorldWar-2.net. "Famous Quotes." 2006. Retrieved September 3, 2008. www.worldwar-2.net/famous-quotes/famousquotes-index.htm.

ABOUT THE AUTHOR

C hristopher LaHurd was born and raised in Tallmadge, just outside of Akron, Ohio. LaHurd has always been fascinated with military history and international affairs. These interests, along with his grandfather's war letters, eventually resulted in this book. LaHurd earned his bachelor of science degree in applied mathematics from the University of Akron and a master of business administration degree from the University of Michigan. He currently resides in Chicago with his family.

Visit us at
www.historypress.net
....
This title is also available as an e-book

CPSIA information can be obtained
at www.ICGtesting.com
Printed in the USA
BVOW06*1044031117
499393BV00017B/19/P